Shadow knitting

Vivian Høxbro

INTERWEAVE PRESS

Shadow knitting

Editors: Lorrie LeJeune, Ann Budd
Technical editor: Jean Lampe
Translator: Carol Rhoades
Designer: Bren Frisch
Production: Samantha L. Thaler
Photo stylist: Ann Swanson
Illustrator: Gayle Ford
Photographer: Joe Coca
Proofreader and indexer: Nancy Arndt

 Interweave Press, Inc.
201 East Fourth Street
Loveland, Colorado 80537-5655 USA
www.interweave.com

Printed in China by R.R. Donnelley

Library of Congress Cataloging-in-Publication Data

Høxbro, Vivian.
  Shadow knitting / Vivian Høxbro.
      p. cm.
  Includes index.
  ISBN 1-931499-41-1
  1. Knitting. 2. Knitting--Patterns. I. Title.
  TT820.H817 2004
  746.43'2--dc22

                          2004001075

10 9 8 7 6 5 4 3 2 1

Table of contents

4 PREFACE

    Origins of Shadow Knitting 4

6 INTRODUCTION

    About Shadow Knitting 6

    Tips—Before You Knit 11

15 PROJECTS

Shadow Knitting for Everyone

    Potholders 16

    Fur Heart Bag 20

    Button Heart Bag 24

    Classic Cross Pillow 28

    Diagonal Cross Pillow 32

    Matching Hat and Scarf 38

    Heart Top 42

    Wing Shawls 48

        Small Shawl 50

        Triangles Shawl 52

        Diagonal Stripes Shawl 56

    Squared Top 64

    Block Pullover 72

    Tone-on-Tone Sweaters 78

        For Her 78

        For Him 84

    Rainbow Jacket 88

Advanced Projects

    Ocean Vest 94

    Triangle Top 102

    Collared Jacket 110

    Sawtooth Sweater 120

    Nihon Japanese Kimono 126

134 ABBREVIATIONS

135 TECHNIQUES

141 RESOURCES

143 INDEX

PrefACE

Origins of

Many years ago, when I worked for *Ugebladet Søndag,* Copenhagen's Sunday newspaper, I found an old knitting article in the archives. It featured a lovely jacket made in "Japanese Fine Knitting." The pattern was simple, but unusual, and came from a little booklet written by Mieko Yano, a Japanese handicraft teacher. The booklet had been translated from Swedish by Karen Lindberg who had studied and become enthusiastic about the technique.

Some years later, while visiting the Sewing Festival exhibition in Malmö, Sweden, I saw examples of Maria Gustafsson's "Optical Knitting." It was identical to "Japanese Fine Knitting." I contacted Maria, who very generously shared with me her vast experience in optical knitting, and loaned me her materials and pictures of her fine work. Maria also sent me the story of how she saw optical knitting for the first time and how her curiosity was awakened. Both her path and mine led to Japan.

A year and a half ago, a beautifully edited version of my book *Domino Knitting* was published in Japan. Following a rather

shadow knitting

complex path of contacts, my editor, Akiyo Murono, eventually pointed me to the booklet by Mieko Yano. My search had come full circle.

While working on my knitwear collection, I realized that I must take up this exciting and somewhat mysterious knitting technique. When a friend suggested calling it "Shadow Knitting," I was delighted. "Shadow Knitting" is the perfect name since it very accurately describes the special look of the technique. The right-side ridges cast a shadow pattern that changes when the wearer moves. My first design was a jacket called *Japan*. With my curiosity piqued, I developed the technique further with *Bumblebee, Zebra,* and *Shadows*. (You can find these designs and more on my website: www.viv.dk.)

My shadow-knitted pieces generated a great deal of interest, and eventually Marilyn Murphy from Interweave Press

encouraged me to write this book. I began writing and discovered that the way was lighted. Thank you, Marilyn, for your encouragement. In 2002, while visiting in Loveland, Colorado, I met some of the employees of Interweave Press. They were very inspiring and helpful, and I am very thankful to all of them.

For long periods in the winter, I am unable to knit, so it has been a fantastic experience to have my knitting friends literally take up the needles for me. Of course, this has also led to all sorts of good knitting chats, and lots of cups of coffee. Many, many thanks to Else Nielsen, Kirsten Jensen, Helle Sørensen, and Else Troelsen. Without all of you, there would not be a book. Finally, thank you to Akiyo Murono, Taeko Hatta, and Maria Gustafsson for your help and inspiration.

I have designed all the patterns and instructions contained in this book. Now they are yours to enjoy, so please knit them. My very best wishes for much knitting pleasure!

Vivian Høxbro

A Japanese book on "Hidden Patterns," was the inspiration for **Shadow Knitting.**

introductioN

ABOUT SHADOW KNITTING

Shadow knitting is very simple in principle. It uses just two stitch patterns, garter stitch and stockinette stitch, and the patterning is minimalistic. If you look at a shadow-knit garment directly from the front, it is difficult to see the pattern, but when the person wearing the garment moves, the pattern becomes visible. It almost seems like magic.

In shadow knitting, the right side of the work always begins with a knit row. The patterning is worked on the wrong side, alternating two rows worked in a dark color and two rows worked in a light color (or vice versa, two rows worked in a light color followed by two rows worked in a dark color). The pattern itself is formed on the right side by the purl ridges. Working knit stitches on the wrong-side rows creates the right-side purl ridges. An American knitter once told me that she saw it as "up-hill" (ridges) and "down-dale" (smooth). This is an excellent way to describe the shadow-producing texture. Although the principles of shadow knitting are simple, the results are unusual and exciting. The patterning is subtler than that of multicolored knitting (Fair Isle, jacquard, Norwegian pattern knitting, intarsia, etc.), and a large piece must be knitted for the shadow patterns to show. At the beginning, your knitting will look like plain old stripes, but don't worry; give it a few inches and the magic will happen!

Three views of a shadow-knitted circle pattern. The pattern is more visible at some angles, and nearly disappears at others.

How Shadow-Knitted Patterns Are Formed

The principles of shadow knitting may be summed up in a few simple statements:

- Shadow knitting always uses at least two colors—one dark and one light.
- Shadow knitting is always worked with only one color at a time—the rows of knitting alternate between two rows of a dark color and two row of a light color.
- Shadow knitting is always worked with knit and purl stitches.
- On right-side rows, all of the stitches are knitted.
- On wrong-side rows, the same color is used as for the previous right-side row, and the stitches are either knitted or purled based on a chart or text instructions.

It is not easy to see the shadow pattern while you're knitting it because it is worked on the wrong side. To build the pattern successfully while working on the wrong side, you'll need to use a system of markers. Following a charted pattern, place the markers at the points where the pattern shifts from knit stitches to purl stitches, and vice versa. Sometimes you may have many, many markers on your needle, but with those markers in place, you'll be nearly able to work the pattern on wrong-side rows with your eyes closed. For more about markers, see Using Markers on page 12.

The Basic Shadow Patterns

Shadow knitting begins with two basic patterns. *Basic Pattern 1* has light ridges on a dark stockinette background; *Basic Pattern 2* has dark ridges on a light stockinette background. The row-by-row instructions for these two basic patterns are at right.

Basic Pattern 1

Row 1 : *(RS) With dark yarn (D), knit.*
Row 2: *(WS) With D, purl.*
Row 3: *(RS) With light yarn (L), knit.*
Row 4: *(WS) With L, knit. This row will form light-colored ridges on the right side of the work.*
Repeat Rows 1–4 for pattern.

Basic Pattern 2

Row 1: *(RS) With L, knit.*
Row 2: *(WS) With L, purl.*
Row 3: *(RS) With D, knit.*
Row 4: *(WS) With D, knit. This row will form dark-colored ridges on the right side of the work*
Repeat Rows 1–4 for pattern.

If you combine Basic Patterns 1 and 2 in the right way, you'll create a shadow pattern! For example, when Basic Patterns 1 and 2 are combined so that the light and dark colors alternate with each other in blocks, as shown at the top of page 9, the shift in the purl ridges creates a pattern. If you alternate 10 stitches of Basic Pattern 1 with 10 stitches of Basic Pattern 2, you get a pattern I call *Stripes*. This pattern is used for the pot holders on page 16, as well as other designs in this book.

You can also shift light and dark rows diagonally to one side or the other, or switch them from the right side to the wrong side to get a totally different result. The chart at the bottom of page 8 shows what happens when the pattern is shifted two stitches to the right every four rows. This pattern is called *Right Diagonal 2R,* and could, for example, be quite dashing on the front of a sweater, vest, or buttoned top. The Sawtooth Sweater on page 120 has this type of diagonal line repeated in stripes throughout the entire garment.

Rearranging the knit and purl stitches in this way can create an endless number of different patterns. To maximize their visual impact, shadow-knitted patterns should be as large and as simple as possible.

Charts

The shadow-knitting charts may look complicated, but they are easy to read once you understand how. Each square represents one stitch of one row. Symbols within the squares indicate how that particular stitch is to be worked. Unless otherwise instructed, begin a chart at the lower right corner. The box in this corner represents the first stitch of the first charted right-side (RS) row. Follow the chart from right to left for stitches on right-side rows. The second row of squares represents the first wrong-side (WS) row. Follow the chart from left to right for stitches on wrong-side rows. Unless otherwise specified, all odd-numbered rows are right-side rows and are read from right to left; all even-numbered rows are wrong-side rows and are read from left to right. The symbols in the charts represent the stitches as they appear when looking at the right side of the knitting. Pattern repeats are groups of stitches that are repeated vertically and/or horizontally. In this book, the pattern repeats are outlined in red. If necessary, additional instructions are written beneath the charts to give more specific details.

Each chart is accompanied by a key that identifies the symbols in the boxes. These symbols denote the colors to use and whether to knit or purl, or treat the stitch in some special way. Be aware that the same symbol may represent different actions on different charts. Therefore, it's important to study the key to learn what the symbols represent before you begin.

To familiarize yourself with how to read shadow-knitting charts, look at the two charts above while you follow the row-by-row instructions on page 10.

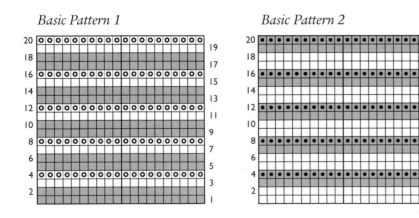

Basic Pattern 1 *Basic Pattern 2*

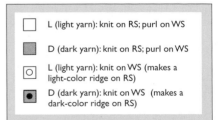

L (light yarn): knit on RS; purl on WS

D (dark yarn): knit on RS; purl on WS

L (light yarn): knit on WS (makes a light-color ridge on RS)

D (dark yarn): knit on WS (makes a dark-color ridge on RS)

Basic Pattern 1

Basic Pattern 2

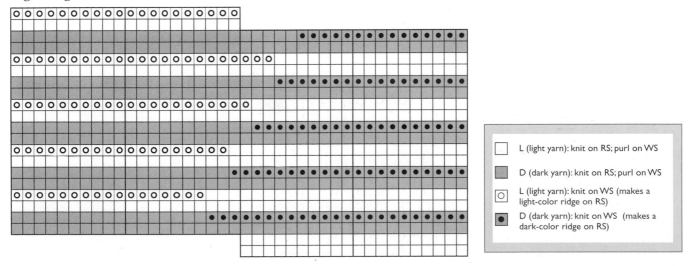

Position Basic Pattern 1 and Basic Pattern 2 next to each other to form a stripe pattern. Shift the stripes to the left or right to form diagonals.

Stripes

Right Diagonal 2R

	L (light yarn): knit on RS; purl on WS
	D (dark yarn): knit on RS; purl on WS
○	L (light yarn): knit on WS (makes a light-color ridge on RS)
●	D (dark yarn): knit on WS (makes a dark-color ridge on RS)

To work the chart for *Basic Pattern 1,* begin at the lower right-hand corner and work as follows:

Row 1: (RS) With dark yarn (D), knit.
Row 2: (WS) With D, purl.
Row 3: (RS) With light yarn (L), knit.
Row 4: (WS) With L, knit. This row will form light-colored purl ridges on the RS of work.
Repeat Rows 1–4 for pattern.

To work the chart for *Basic Pattern 2,* begin at the lower right-hand corner and work as follows:

Row 1: (RS) With L, knit.
Row 2: (WS) With L, purl.
Row 3: (RS) With D, knit.
Row 4: (WS) With D, knit. This row will form dark-colored purl ridges on the RS of work.
Repeat Rows 1–4 for pattern.

Color

The shadow patterns are sharpest when they are knitted with dark and light colors. Black and white yarns are a sure success, but you can also work with colors and paler contrasting shades. If you're not sure the colors you've chosen will work together, experiment first on a small project such as a potholder.

You can also experiment with positive and negative space, that is, making the motifs or the space between them light or dark. Let's say you choose a pattern of triangles on a contrasting background. If you knit

Dark triangles on a light background appear to fade into this top. (Instructions for this top begin on page 102.)

the triangles with a light color, they will pop out from the dark background. However, if you make the triangles dark and the background light, the triangles will appear to fade back into the piece, and the area between the triangles will be more prominent.

Yarns

Any yarn can be used for shadow knitting, but in my experience, some yarns work better than others. A round, tightly spun, cotton yarn is the best choice for razor-sharp shadow patterns. In fact, the rounder and firmer the yarn, the more clearly the pattern will stand out. The pot holders on page 16 are good examples of a sharp pattern.

For many of the designs in this book, I recommend using Harrisville Designs New England Shetland (100% wool). The shadow patterns do not stand out quite as sharply with this yarn as they do with cotton, but the soft yarns have a chenille-like quality that looks quite elegant.

If you knit the same designs with Tiur from Dalegarn (60% mohair, 40% wool), the patterns will appear more distinct than with the Harrisville yarn. The green version of the Nihon Kimono Jacket on page 126 is made with Tiur, with quite nice results. Do not be afraid to experiment with a variety of yarns. Whether sharply defined, or more subtly contrasting, any shadow-knitted garment will be beautiful and elegant.

Gauge

Before beginning a project, always make a gauge swatch and measure it carefully! Shadow knitting must be worked more tightly than normal knitting for the pattern to appear properly. If you want to be certain that your work will be the desired size, your gauge swatch is extremely important. Most of the larger garments in this book are worked from side to side. Jackets or tops knitted in this way tend to draw up somewhat in length, so making an accurate gauge swatch is crucial for calculating a proper fit.

Make your gauge swatch larger than the number of stitches and rows specified for the gauge. For example, cast on 6 stitches more than the gauge specified for a 4″ (10-cm) width in the pattern—3 extra stitches on each side. Work 5 rows in garter stitch (knit every row), then working the 3 extra stitches at each side in garter stitch, work the center stitches in the shadow pattern for 4″ (10 cm), work garter stitch for 5 more rows, then bind off all the stitches.

To measure the gauge, lay the swatch flat on a hard surface and smooth out the edges. With a wooden or metal ruler, measure 4″ (10 cm) across the width of the pattern area (don't include the extra side stitches in your measurement) and count the number of stitches in a 4″ (10-cm) width. Then measure 4″ (10 cm) along the length of the pattern area (excluding the garter-stitch borders) and count the number of rows in a 4″ (10 cm) length. If your swatch has too few stitches or rows for the required gauge, your stitches are too large, and you should try again using a smaller needle size. If there are too many stitches in the swatch, your stitches are too small; try again using a larger needle.

TIPS—BEFORE YOU KNIT

Shadow knitting utilizes a few specialized techniques such as edge stitches, proper use of markers, and weaving in ends. Familiarize yourself with them before you knit to ensure a beautiful garment.

Edge Stitches

Your garment will be easier to finish and will look more professional if the edges are even and smooth. Except for the very first row after casting on, always slip the first stitch as if to knit (kwise) and purl the last stitch in every row. This will form chain stitches along the side edges, as shown below. For the very first row after the cast-on, the edge stitches are worked as for the rest of the row, or as specified in the instructions.

Be sure that the edge stitches on each side of your piece have the same elasticity. On the right side, where the color changes occur, the knitting may become too tight. On the wrong side it may become too loose. To prevent this, keep your tension a little looser when beginning each right-side

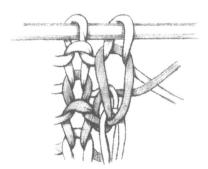

Chain links form along the side edges.

The stitches along the color-change edge on the wrong side tend to be a bit loose.

The stitches along the color-change edge on the right side tend to be a little tight.

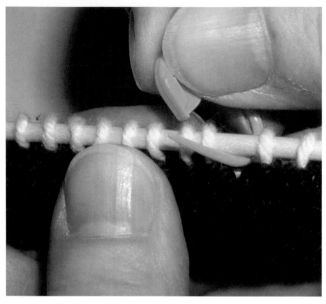

Use markers (removable lock-ring markers are shown here) to designate boundaries between knit and purl stitches of the same color.

Use different colors of markers to keep track of complex patterns.

row, and pull the yarn a little tighter after the edge stitch on the wrong-side row. Re-establish edge stitches during armhole and neckline shaping, unless otherwise instructed.

Color Changes

In shadow knitting, color changes are always made on right-side rows and the color not in use is carried along the side edge. For a neat finish, the yarns must be twisted around each other at the color change, before working the first stitch with the new color. To twist the yarns, drop the old color and pick up the new color from beneath the old.

Extending the Pattern over Cast-On Stitches

Many of the designs in this book are worked side to side or sleeve to sleeve. The sleeve and neck shaping on this type of sweater construction requires that stitches be cast on at the end or beginning of some rows. On the following row these new stitches must be worked into the established pattern. When this happens, it's important to maintain the integrity of the shadow-knitting pattern. After casting on the new stitches, be sure to extend the pattern (either mentally or on paper) across the new stitches and note the point on the chart where you'll turn and begin to work back. By doing this, you'll be able to seamlessly continue the pattern into the existing stitches.

Using Markers

Markers are a necessity in shadow knitting. Lock-ring markers, which look and function like safety pins, are easy to put on and take off—especially in the middle of a row. Other types of markers can be used, but they can be difficult to adjust while you knit. You can also use cotton thread, which can be woven in and out of the piece as a marker. If you want to use thread, be sure it is about 8″ (20 cm) long so that you'll be sure to notice it as you work.

Place lock-ring markers on the needles so that they open toward the right side of the knitting, as shown here. After working right-side rows, place (or move) the markers as specified in the instructions or as indicated on the chart. The markers will alert you to when you should switch from knit stitches to purl stitches and vice versa on wrong-side rows. Because all of the stitches are always knitted on right-side rows, just slip the markers from the left needle to the right needle when you come to them on these rows. For example, let's say you're working a pattern that alternates knit and purl stitches every 10 stitches. You would place a marker after every 10th stitch (where the stitches change from knit to purl and vice versa). Let's also say that on wrong-side rows the first 10 stitches are purled. To work the pattern, you'd purl to the first marker, slip the marker from the left needle to the right needle, knit to the next marker, slip the marker, purl to the next marker, slip the marker, and so on to the end of the row. On the following right-side row, you'd just knit every stitch, slipping the markers when you come to them. For more complicated patterns that involve multiple colors, use markers of different colors to help you keep track of changes in color as well as changes between knit and purl stitches.

Weaving in Ends

Save yourself time at the end of the project by weaving in the yarn ends as you work. To weave in ends while working the Continental style of knitting (yarn held in the left hand), hold both yarns over the index finger and middle finger of your left hand, just as you would for knitting two-color patterns, as shown in the two illustrations above right. In these illustrations, the new color is shown as dark and the old color is shown as light. Place the new color (dark) closest to the tip of the index finger, and the old color in front of the new color, closer to the main knuckle.

Step 1: Insert the needle under the old color, and catch the new color, knitting the next stitch as usual.

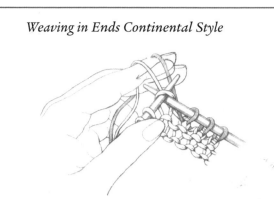

Weaving in Ends Continental Style

Step 1: *Insert needle under old color, catch new color, and knit next stitch as usual.*

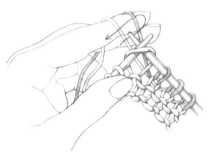

Step 2: *Insert needle over old color, knit the stitch with new color as usual.*

Weaving in Ends American/English Style

Bring old yarn forward and over right needle tip from back to front (as illustrated), knit the new stitch, dropping old stitch and old yarn off the needle as you do so, then knit the next stitch as usual.

Step 2: Insert the needle over the old color, knit the stitch with the new color as usual.

Repeat Steps 1 and 2 for several stitches.

To weave in ends while working the American/English style of knitting (yarn held in the right hand), you'll need to hold one yarn in each hand.

Step 1: Place the old yarn (shown as the light yarn in the illustration at the bottom of page 13) in the left hand and across the left index finger, bringing the old yarn forward and over the right needle tip from back to front. With the new yarn (shown as dark) in the right hand, knit the next stitch, dropping the old stitch and the old yarn off the needle as you pull through the new stitch loop.

Step 2: Knit the next stitch with the new yarn as usual.

Repeat Steps 1 and 2 for several stitches.

After weaving in the ends for several stitches, let the yarn tails hang and continue to work a few more rows so that the woven-in ends can relax into the knitting. Then go back and cut the tails, leaving about ¼" (1 cm) hanging. If you cut the ends closer than that, they may work through to the right side when the garment is washed.

Determining Your Ideal Size

Because garment sizes can be variable and sometimes arbitrary, it's often smarter to knit to fit a particular measurement. Go to your closet or wardrobe and find a sweater that fits you well and is similar to the one you want to design and knit. I call this a measurement sweater. Lay the sweater out flat without pulling or stretching the shape. Measure the width straight across at the underarms, the body length from shoulder to hem, the sleeve length, and the sleeve width at both top and bottom. Write these measurements down, and then compare them to the numbers on the garment schematic provided in this book. Once you've made your comparisons, you can then select the size you want to knit. Don't be surprised if it's not what you expected! You can also make alterations (such as adding or subtracting a few inches to sleeves or the body) at this stage. Just remember to recalculate the number of rows in your pattern if you make such changes.

Counting Rows and Ridges

When counting rows in shadow knitting, remember that each ridge represents four rows of knitting—three rows of stockinette stitch followed by one garter ridge. When counting rows, simply count the number of ridges and multiply by four.

Joining Stitches for Knitting Circularly

When knitting circularly or "in the round," you must join both ends of the work. Using a circular needle (or set of four or five double-pointed needles), arrange the work so that the end of the cast-on row (or last row worked if joining at a place other than the cast-on) is on the right-hand side. The working yarn will also be at this side. Taking care not to twist the stitches on the needles, place a stitch marker on the right-hand needle to mark the beginning of the round, then knit the first stitch on the left-hand needle. Be sure to tension the stitch so that it is not too loose.

Projects

Shadow Knitting for Everyone
  Pot Holders
  Fur Heart Bag
  Button Heart Bag
  Classic Cross Pillow
  Diagonal Cross Pillow
  Matching Hat and Scarf
  Heart Top
  Wing Shawls
    Small Shawl
    Triangles Shawl
    Diagonal Stripes Shawl
  Squared Top
  Block Pullover
  Tone-on-Tone Sweaters
    For Her
    For Him
  Rainbow Jacket

Advanced Projects
  Ocean Vest
  Triangle Top
  Collared Jacket
  Sawtooth Sweater
  Nihon Japanese Kimono

FINISHED SIZE

8¾" (22 cm) wide and 8¾" (22 cm) long.

YARN

DK-weight yarn. Each pot holder requires about 55 yd [50 m] each of dark yarn (D) and light yarn (L).

We suggest Rowan Handknit DK Cotton (100% cotton; 93 yd [85 m]/50 g): 1 ball each of black (D) and white (L).

NEEDLES

US size 4 (3.5 mm): straight. Adjust needle size if necessary to obtain the correct gauge.

NOTIONS

Markers (m); tapestry needle.

GAUGE

21½ stitches and 37 rows = 4" (10 cm) in charted pattern.

POT HOLDERS

Pot holders are excellent first shadow-knitting projects. They are small and easily completed, and by making one or two, you'll learn exactly how shadow patterns work.

NOTES

Before beginning, review Tips—Before you Knit, pages 11–14; Abbreviations, page 134; and Techniques, pages 135–140.

The charts for this project are on page 18. To become familiar with the charted pattern, follow the text instructions and compare them with the charts. The section inside the chart repeat frame (red lines) is one pattern repeat of 20 sts and 4 rows, and is worked twice over 40 sts. The chart does not include the upper and lower borders, or the 4 edge stitches at each side.

FIRST POT HOLDER

With dark yarn (D), CO 48 sts—40 patt sts plus 4 edge sts each side.

Bottom border

Row 1: (WS) Knit to last st, p1.
Rows 2, 3, 4, and 5: (RS) Sl 1 kwise, knit to last st, p1.
There will be a total of 5 rows and 3 ridges on the RS.

Body

Row 6: (RS; Row 1 of Pot Holder 1 chart on page 18) Join light yarn (L), sl 1 kwise, knit to last st, p1.

Place a stitch marker (pm) inside the outermost 4 border sts on each side edge of the pot holder, then pm between every 10 sts as indicated on the chart, with 10 sts between markers. When you come to the markers on subsequent rows, slip them from left needle to right needle (sl m).

Row 7: (WS; Row 2 of chart) With L, sl 1 kwise, k3, sl m, (these 4 edge sts and first marker are not shown on chart), *purl to next marker (these sts will appear as knit sts on the RS), sl m, knit to next marker (these sts will appear as purl ridges on the RS); rep from * to last marker, end k3, p1 (the last marker and 4 edge sts are not shown on chart).

Row 8: (RS; Row 3 of chart) With D, sl 1 kwise, knit to last st (slipping markers as you go), p1.

Row 9: (WS; Row 4 of chart) With D, sl 1 kwise, knit to marker (edge sts), sl m,

*knit to next marker (these sts will appear as purl ridges on the RS), sl m, purl to next marker (these sts will appear as knit sts on RS), sl m; rep from *, end k3, p1 (edge sts).

Rep Rows 6–9 until pot holder is almost square (excluding height of lower border). Work 2 rows with L as shown above the repeat frame on Pot Holder 1 chart.

Top border

With D, work 5 rows as for bottom border. With WS facing, BO all but last 3 sts.

FINISHING

Weave in loose ends to WS.

Pot Holder 1

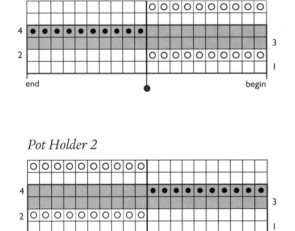

Hanging loop: Cont on rem 3 sts as foll:

Row 1: With D, sl 1 kwise, k1, p1.

Rep Row 1 until loop is 3″ (7.5 cm) long, or desired length. BO all sts. Fold loop in half towards the WS. With D threaded on tapestry needle, sew end of loop neatly to corner edge of BO.

SECOND POT HOLDER

The pattern in this pot holder is a mirror image of the pattern in the first pot holder. Work as for first pot holder, but follow Pot Holder 2 chart instead of Pot Holder 1 chart.

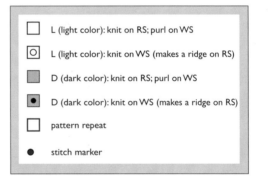

Pot Holder 2

FINISHED SIZE

12¾" (32.5 cm) wide and 13¼" (33.5 cm) long.

YARN

Bulky yarn. Bag requires about 275 yd (250 m) of dark yarn (D) and 100 yd (90 m) of light yarn (L). We used HP Gruppen Cosy Wool (100% wool; 137 yd [125 m]/100 g): #84 dark mauve (D), 2 balls; and GGH Yarns Sierra (77% wool, 23% polyamid; 50 yd [45 m]/ 50 g): #09 brown/mauve/ rose (L), 2 balls.

NEEDLES

US size 10 (6 mm): straight. Adjust needle size if necessary to obtain the correct gauge.

NOTIONS

Markers (m); strip of fake fur fabric about 2" (5 cm) wide and 49¼" (125 cm) long; tapestry needle; sewing needle; sewing thread to coordinate with fur fabric; straight pins; lining fabric twice the bag dimensions plus ½" (1.3 cm) for seam allowances; sewing machine and 1 yd (91.5 cm) grosgrain ribbon, slightly narrower than width of shoulder strap (optional).

GAUGE

14 sts and 25 rows = 4" (10 cm) in charted pattern.

FUR HEART BAG

....

Knit two square swatches using bulky yarn and big needles, rotate 90 degrees, sew them together, apply the trim, attach the strap handle, and voilà! You have a smart bag.

NOTES

Before beginning, review Tips—Before You Knit, pages 11–14; Abbreviations, page 134; Techniques, pages 135–140.

The chart for this project is on page 23. It is 40 stitches wide and 74 rows long; it does not include the edge stitches or border rows.

The heart motif is worked sideways; after the knitting is completed, the piece is turned 90 degrees to bring the purl ridges vertical and the heart motif into the correct orientation.

FRONT

With D, CO 44 sts—40 pattern sts plus 2 edge sts each side.

First Border
Row 1: (WS) With D, knit to last st, p1.
Row 2: (RS) With D, sl 1 kwise, knit to last st, p1.

Row 3: (WS) With D, sl 1 kwise, knit to last st, p1.

Body
Row 1: (RS) With L, sl 1 kwise, k1 (2 edge sts), work next 40 sts according to Row 1 of Heart chart (page 23), end k1, p1 (2 edge sts).
Row 2: (WS) With L, sl 1 kwise, k1 (edge sts), work next 40 sts according to Row 2 of chart, end k1, p1 (edge sts).
Working 2 edge sts at each end of needle as established, cont working center 40 sts through Row 74 of chart.

Second Border
Rows 1 and 3: (RS) With D, sl 1 kwise, knit to last st, p1.
Row 2: (WS) With D, sl 1 kwise, knit to last st, p1.
With D and WS facing, BO all sts kwise.

BACK

Work as front.

FINISHING

Fur decoration: With sewing needle and thread, baste fur strip securely around heart motif on bag front, carefully following the knitted heart outline formed by light ridges on dark background.

Shoulder strap: With D, CO 9 sts. Working the first and last sts every row as edge sts (see page 11), work center 7 sts in garter st until strap measures about 28"–32" (71 cm–81.5 cm), or desired length. BO all sts. Sew shoulder strap firmly to WS of bag at each side seam. To stabilize shoulder strap and prevent stretching, sew optional grosgrain ribbon to WS of strap.

Seams: Turn front and back each 90 degrees so heart motifs are upright and purl ridges are vertical. With D threaded on a tapestry needle and using a whipstitch (see Techniques, page 140), sew sides and lower edges of front to back. Weave in loose ends to WS.

Lining: Cut lining fabric to match bag circumference plus ½" (1.3 cm) seam allowance on all four sides. Pin RS of lining fabric tog, leaving top edge open. With sewing machine (or by hand), sew both side and bottom edges. Insert lining into bag with WS of lining facing WS of bag. Fold top edge seam allowance of lining to WS and pin lining in place around top edge of bag, about ½" (1.3 cm) down from top edge of knitting. With matching thread and sewing needle, sew lining neatly in place. Remove all pins.

Heart

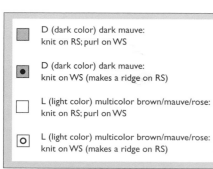

D (dark color) dark mauve:
knit on RS; purl on WS

D (dark color) dark mauve:
knit on WS (makes a ridge on RS)

L (light color) multicolor brown/mauve/rose:
knit on RS; purl on WS

L (light color) multicolor brown/mauve/rose:
knit on WS (makes a ridge on RS)

73
71
69
67
65
63
61
59
57
55
53
51
49
47
45
43
41
39
37
35
33
31
29
27
25
23
21
19
17
15
13
11
9
7
5
3
1

end

begin

FINISHED SIZE

8¾" (22 cm) wide and 9½" (24 cm) long.

YARN

Worsted-weight yarn. Bag requires about 99 yd (90 m) each of two light colors and two dark colors.
We suggest Rowan All Seasons Cotton (50% cotton, 50% acrylic; 99 yd [90 m]/ 50 g): navy blue (D1), gray-blue (D2), yellow (L1), and mocha (L2), 1 ball each.

NEEDLES

US size 4 (3.5 mm): straight. Adjust needle size if necessary to obtain the correct gauge.

NOTIONS

Markers (m); tapestry needle; fourteen ½" (1.3-cm) buttons; sharp-point sewing needle; matching sewing thread; straight pins; lining fabric twice the bag dimensions plus ½" (1.3 cm) for seam allowances; sewing machine (optional).

GAUGE

19 sts and 34 rows = 4" (10 cm) in charted pattern.

BUTTON HEART BAG

Here is a simple, colorful bag that's quick to make. This bag is the perfect size for a child, or to hold a small craft project.

NOTES

Before beginning, review Tips—Before You Knit, pages 11–14; Abbreviations, page 134; Techniques, pages 135–140.

The charts for this project are on page 27. Each chart is 40 stitches wide and 74 rows long; the charts do not include the edge stitches or border rows.

The colors on the front and back of the bag are reversed.

FRONT

With D1, CO 44 sts—40 patt sts plus 2 edge sts each side.

First Border
Row 1: (WS) With D1, knit to last st, p1.
Row 2: (RS) With D1, sl 1 kwise, knit to last st, p1.
Row 3: (WS) With D1, sl 1 kwise, knit to last st, p1.

Body
Row 1: (RS) With L2, sl 1 kwise, k1 (2 edge sts), work next 40 sts according to Row 1 of Bag Front chart (page 27), end k1, p1 (2 edge sts).

Row 2: (WS) With L2, sl 1 kwise, k1 (edge sts), work next 40 sts according to Row 2 of chart, end k1, p1 (edge sts). Working 2 edge sts at each end of needle as established, work center 40 sts through Row 74 of chart.

Second Border
Rows 1 and 3: (RS) With D2, sl 1 kwise, knit to last st, p1.
Row 2: (WS) With D2, sl 1 kwise, knit to last st, p1.
With WS facing and D2, BO all sts kwise.

BACK

With D2, CO 44 sts—40 patt sts plus 2 edge sts each side.

First Border
Row 1: (WS) With D2, knit to last st, p1.
Row 2: (RS) With D2, sl 1 kwise, knit to last st, p1.
Row 3: (WS) With D2, sl 1 kwise, knit to last st, p1.

Body
Row 1: (RS) With L1, sl 1 kwise, k1 (2 edge sts), work next 40 sts according to Row 1 of Bag Back chart, end k1, p1 (2 edge sts).

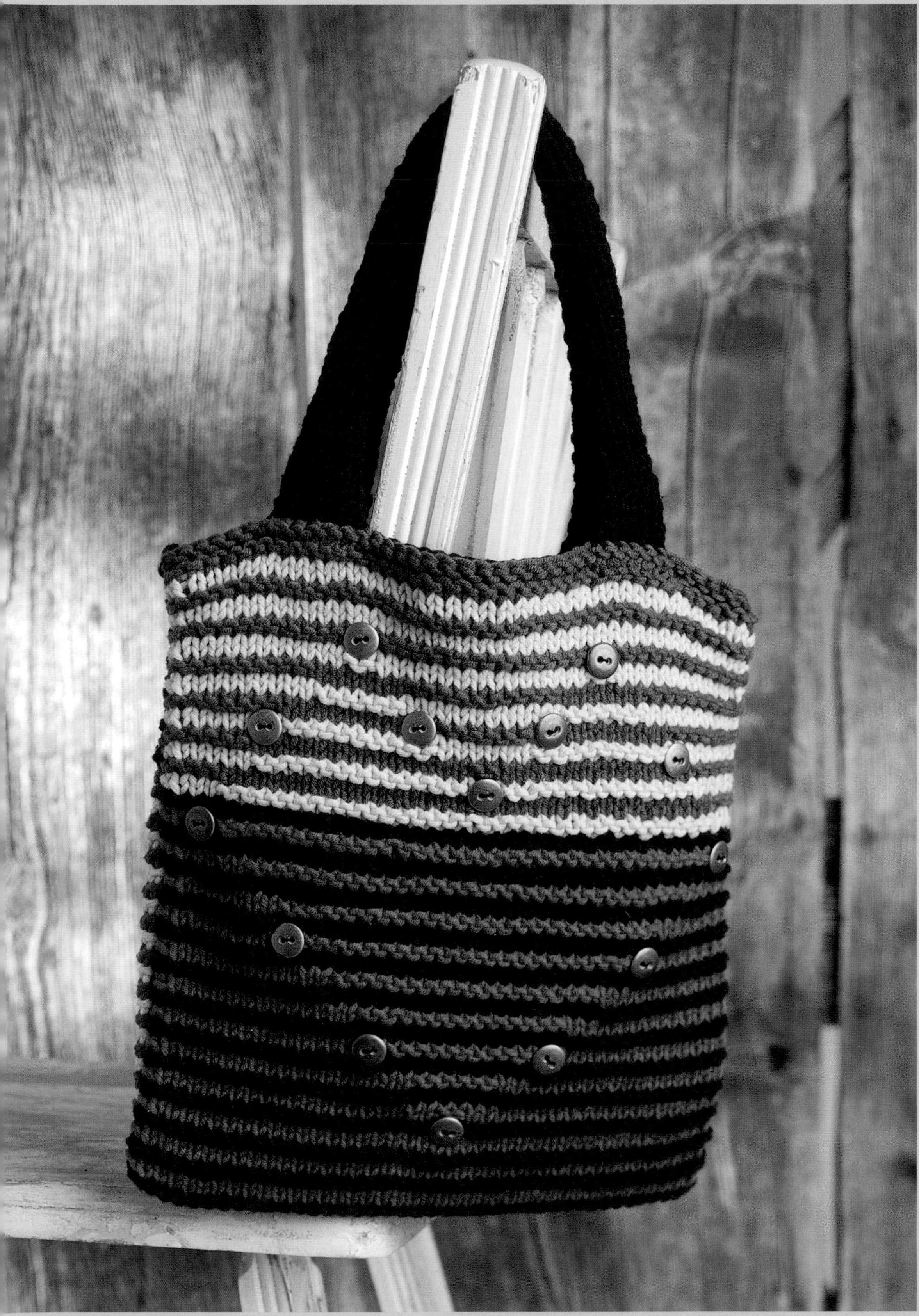

Row 2: (WS) With L1, sl 1 kwise, k1 (edge sts), work next 40 sts according to Row 2 of chart, end k1, p1 (edge sts).

Working 2 edge sts at each end of needle as established, work center 40 sts through Row 74 of chart.

Second Border

Rows 1 and 3: (RS) With D1, sl 1 kwise, knit to last st, p1.
Row 2: (WS) With D1, sl 1 kwise, knit to last st, p1.
With WS facing and D1, BO all sts kwise.

FINISHING

Buttons: With matching thread and sewing needle, sew 14 buttons around the heart motif (dark ridges on a light background) on front as shown in photo below.

Seams: With D1 threaded on a tapestry needle and using the mattress st (see Techniques, page 140), sew front to back along sides and use the invisible hori-zontal seam (see Techniques, page 139) to sew base. Weave in loose ends on WS.

Handles: (make 2) With D1, CO 9 sts. Work all sts in St st (knit on RS; purl on WS) for 13" (33 cm)—edges will curl to WS. Position handle edges about 2" (5 cm) in from side seams and pin in place. With D1 threaded on a tapestry needle, sew handle to WS of bag. Join second handle to other side of bag the same way.

Lining: Cut lining fabric to match bag dimensions, plus ½" (1.3-cm) seam allowance around all four sides. Pin RS of lining tog, leaving top edge open. With sewing machine (or by hand) and matching thread, sew both side seams and across bottom edge. Insert lining into bag with WS of lining facing WS of bag. Fold top edge seam allowance of lining to WS and pin lining in place around top edge of bag, about ½" (1.3 cm) down from top edge of knitting. With sewing needle and matching thread, sew lining in place. Remove all pins.

Bag Front

Bag Back

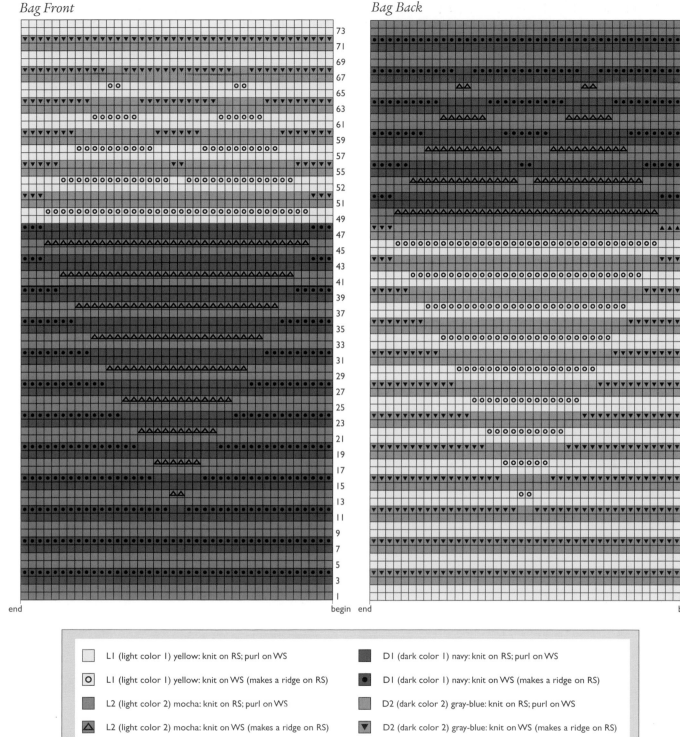

end   begin   end   begin

	L1 (light color 1) yellow: knit on RS; purl on WS		D1 (dark color 1) navy: knit on RS; purl on WS
⊙	L1 (light color 1) yellow: knit on WS (makes a ridge on RS)	●	D1 (dark color 1) navy: knit on WS (makes a ridge on RS)
	L2 (light color 2) mocha: knit on RS; purl on WS		D2 (dark color 2) gray-blue: knit on RS; purl on WS
▲	L2 (light color 2) mocha: knit on WS (makes a ridge on RS)	▼	D2 (dark color 2) gray-blue: knit on WS (makes a ridge on RS)

CLASSIC CROSS PILLOW

This pillow features one horizontal and one vertical line, which make up the classic cross. The lines divide the pillows into dark and light areas. Knit the front side of the pillow and sew on a coordinated fabric backing for the other side.

FINISHED SIZE

13" (33 cm) wide and 13½" (34.5 cm) long, including edgings.

YARN

Fingering-weight yarn. Pillow requires about 185 yd (170 m) each of dark (D) and light (L) yarn. We suggest Rowan 4-ply Cotton, (100% cotton; 186 yd [170 m]/50 g): mocha (D) and rust (L), 1 ball each.

NEEDLES

US size 2 (2.75 mm): straight. Adjust needle size if necessary to obtain the correct gauge.

NOTIONS

Markers (m); tapestry needle; fabric for pillow back (about 13" [33 cm] wide by 13½" [34.5 cm] long); 15¾" (40-cm) square pillow form or fiberfill stuffing; sharp-point sewing needle and thread to match backing fabric.

GAUGE

27 sts and 48 rows = 4" (10 cm) in charted pattern.

NOTES

Before beginning, review Tips—Before you Knit, pages 11–14; Abbreviations, page 134; Techniques, pages 135–140.

The charts for this project are on page 30. Each chart is 40 stitches wide and 74 rows long; the charts do not include the edge stitches or border rows. The section inside each of the chart repeat frames (red lines) is one pattern repeat of 20 sts, and is worked twice over 40 sts.

PILLOW

Bottom Border

With D and using the knitted method (see Techniques, page 136), CO 5 sts.
Row 1: (WS) With D, k4, p1.
Row 2: (RS) With L, sl 1 kwise, k3, p1.
Row 3: With L, sl 1 kwise, k3, p1.
Row 4: With D, sl 1 kwise, k3, p1.
Row 5: With D, sl 1 kwise, k3, p1.

Rep Rows 2–5 until there are 89 ridges, ending with a WS row in L. *Next row:* (RS) With D, BO 4 sts kwise—1 st rem. Do not fasten off.

Body

With RS facing, 1 st on needle, and cont with D, pick up and knit 89 more sts along left side of border—90 sts total. *Next row:* (WS) Cont with D, sl 1 kwise, knit to last st, p1 (this will create a row of dark ridges on the RS). Place a marker (pm) after the first 5 sts to denote side border, another marker at the center of the row (after 45 sts) to denote center of chart, and a third marker before the last 5 sts to denote the other side border. Cont as foll:
Row 1: (RS) With L, sl 1 kwise, k4 (5 side border sts; not shown on chart), slip marker (sl m), work next 80 sts according to Row 1 of Lower Pillow chart

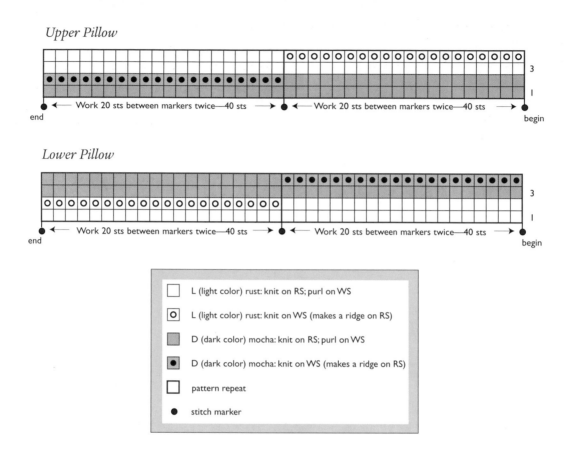

Upper Pillow

← end — Work 20 sts between markers twice—40 sts → ← Work 20 sts between markers twice—40 sts → begin

Lower Pillow

← end — Work 20 sts between markers twice—40 sts → ← Work 20 sts between markers twice—40 sts → begin

L (light color) rust: knit on RS; purl on WS

L (light color) rust: knit on WS (makes a ridge on RS)

D (dark color) mocha: knit on RS; purl on WS

D (dark color) mocha: knit on WS (makes a ridge on RS)

pattern repeat

stitch marker

(note that first 40 sts are worked according to right half of chart and second 40 sts are worked according to left half of chart), sl m, k4, p1 (5 side border sts; not shown on chart).

Row 2: (WS) With L, sl 1 kwise, k4, sl m, work next 80 sts according to Row 2 of chart, sl m, k4, p1.

Row 3: With D, sl 1 kwise, k4, sl m, work next 80 sts according to Row 3 of chart, sl m, k4, p1.

Row 4: With D, sl 1 kwise, k4, sl m, work next 80 sts according to Row 4 of chart, sl m, k4, p1.

Cont in this manner, working 5 side border sts each end of needle (sl 1 kwise, k4 at beg of rows; k4, p1 at end of rows), and working center 80 sts according to Rows 1–4 of chart 18 times total—72 rows total. With L, knit 2 rows—

piece should measure about 6¾" (17 cm), including bottom border. Change to Upper Pillow chart. Cont working first 5 sts and last 5 sts in side border patt as established, work center 80 sts according to Rows 1–4 of chart 18 times total—72 rows; the color ridges will shift so that the right half will have light ridges and the left half will have dark ridges; piece should measure about 6" (15 cm) from beg of Upper Pillow chart.

Top Border

Knit 2 rows with D, slipping the first st kwise and purling the last st of each row to create a row of dark ridges prior to the border that matches the lower half of the pillow. Turn work. With RS facing and using the knitted method,

CO 5 sts with D at beg of row for top border—95 sts. Join border to top of pillow as foll:

Row 1: (RS still facing) With D, sl 1 kwise, k3, p2tog (1 border st and 1 pillow body st). Turn work.

Row 2: (WS) With D, sl 1 kwise, k3, p1.

Row 3: With L, sl 1 kwise, k3, p2tog (the resulting bi-color purl st is minimized in the next row when the first st is slipped knitwise). Turn work.

Row 4: With L, sl 1 kwise, k3, p1.

Rep Rows 1–4 until all pillow body sts have been worked—5 border sts rem. BO rem sts.

FINISHING

Pillow backing: Working around all four sides of the fabric backing, fold under ¾" (2-cm) seam allowance to WS. With WS tog, pin backing to pillow front, leaving the 5-st borders free. With sewing needle and matching thread, sew fabric backing to pillow front, working inside the 5-st borders and leaving an opening about 10" (25.5 cm) along one side. Remove pins.

Weave in loose ends to WS. Insert pillow form or stuff firmly with fiberfill. Sew opening tog to close pillow.

This pillow features diagonal lines that divide the dark and light spaces. Once the edging is knitted, the work almost goes by itself! Knit the front side of the pillow and sew on a coordinated fabric backing for the other side.

FINISHED SIZE

13" (33 cm) wide and 14½" (37 cm) long, including edgings.

YARN

Fingering-weight yarn. Pillow requires about 328 yd (300 m) each of dark (D) and light (L) yarn.
We used HP Gruppen Kick (50% cotton, 50% acrylic; 164 yd [150 m]/50 g): dark olive (D) and yellow-green (L), 2 balls each.

NEEDLES

US size 2 (2.75 mm): straight. Adjust needle size if necessary to obtain the correct gauge.

NOTIONS

Markers (m); tapestry needle; fabric for pillow back, about 13" (33 cm) wide and 14½" (37 cm) tall; 1 pillow form 15¾" (40 cm) wide and 17¾" (45 cm) tall, or polyester fiberfill; sharp-point sewing needle and thread to match backing fabric.

GAUGE

28 sts and 48 rows = 4" (10 cm) in charted pattern.

NOTES

Before beginning, review Tips—Before You Knit, pages 11–14; Abbreviations, page 134; Techniques, pages 135–140.

The charts for this project are on pages 34 and 37. Each chart is 80 stitches wide and 80 rows long; the charts do not include the side border stitches or top and bottom border rows.

PILLOW

Bottom border

With D and using the knitted method (see Techniques, page 136), CO 5 sts.
Row 1: (WS) With D, k4, p1.
Row 2: (RS) With L, sl 1 kwise, k3, p1.
Row 3: With L, sl 1 kwise, k3, p1.
Row 4: With D, sl 1 kwise, k3, p1.
Row 5: With D, sl 1 kwise, k3, p1.
Rep Rows 2–5 until there are 89 ridges, ending with a WS row in L. *Next row:* (RS) With D, BO 4 sts kwise—1 st rem. Do not fasten off.

Body

With RS facing, 1 st on needle, and cont with D, pick up and knit 89 more sts along left side of border—90 sts total.
Next row: (WS) Cont with D, sl 1 kwise, knit to last st, p1 (this will form dark ridges on the RS). Place a marker (pm) after the first 5 sts and another marker before the last 5 sts to denote side borders. Cont as foll:
Row 1: (RS) With L, sl 1 kwise, k4 (5 border sts; not shown on chart), slip marker (sl m), work next 80 sts according to Row 1 of Lower Diagonal chart (page 34), sl m, k4, p1 (5 border sts; not shown on chart).
Row 2: (WS) With L, sl 1 kwise, k4, sl m, work next 80 sts according to Row 2 of chart, sl m, k4, p1.
Row 3: With D, sl 1 kwise, k4, sl m, work next 80 sts according to Row 3 of chart, sl m, k4, p1.

Lower Diagonal

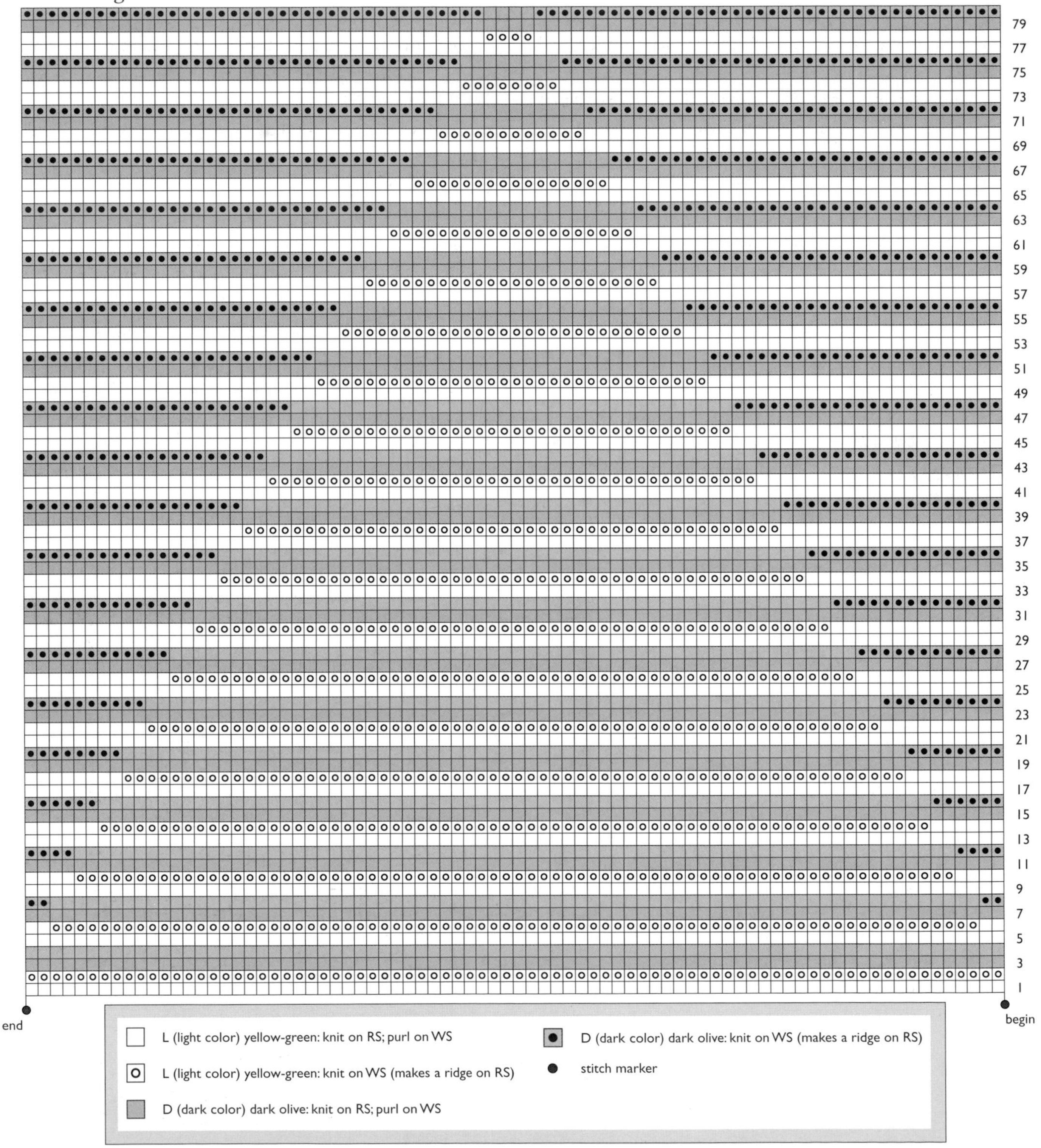

- ☐ L (light color) yellow-green: knit on RS; purl on WS
- ○ L (light color) yellow-green: knit on WS (makes a ridge on RS)
- ■ D (dark color) dark olive: knit on RS; purl on WS
- ● D (dark color) dark olive: knit on WS (makes a ridge on RS)
- ● stitch marker

Row 4: With D, sl 1 kwise, k4, sl m, work next 80 sts according to Row 4 of chart, sl m, k4, p1.

Cont in this manner, working 5 side border sts each end of needle (sl 1 kwise, k4 at beg of rows; k4, p1 at end of rows), and working center 80 sts through Row 80 of chart (increasing the width of the dark ridges on the sides and decreasing the width of the light ridges in the center)— this is the center of the pillow. Change to Upper Diagonal chart (page 37). Cont working the first 5 sts and last 5 sts in side border patt as established, work center 80 sts according to Rows 1–78 of chart.

Top border

Knit 2 rows with D, slipping the first st kwise and purling the last st of each row to create a row of dark ridges prior to the border that matches the lower half of the pillow. Turn work. With RS facing and using the knitted method, CO 5 sts with D at beg of row for top border—95 sts. Join border to top of pillow as foll:

Row 1: (RS still facing) With D, sl 1 kwise, k3, p2tog (1 border st and 1 pillow body st). Turn work.

Row 2: (WS) With D, sl 1 kwise, k3, p1.

Row 3: With L, sl 1 kwise, k3, p2tog (the resulting bi-color purl st is minimized in the next row when the first st is slipped kwise). Turn work.

Row 4: With L, sl 1 kwise, k3, p1.

Rep Rows 1–4 until all pillow body sts have been worked— 5 border sts rem. BO rem sts.

FINISHING

Pillow backing: Working around all four sides of the fabric backing, fold under ¾" (2-cm) seam allowance to WS. With WS tog, pin backing to pillow front, leaving the 5-st border free. With sewing needle and matching thread, sew fabric backing to pillow front, working inside the 5-st borders and leaving an opening about 10" (25.5 cm) along one side. Remove pins.

Weave in loose ends to WS. Insert pillow form or stuff firmly with fiberfill. Sew opening tog to close pillow.

Upper Diagonal

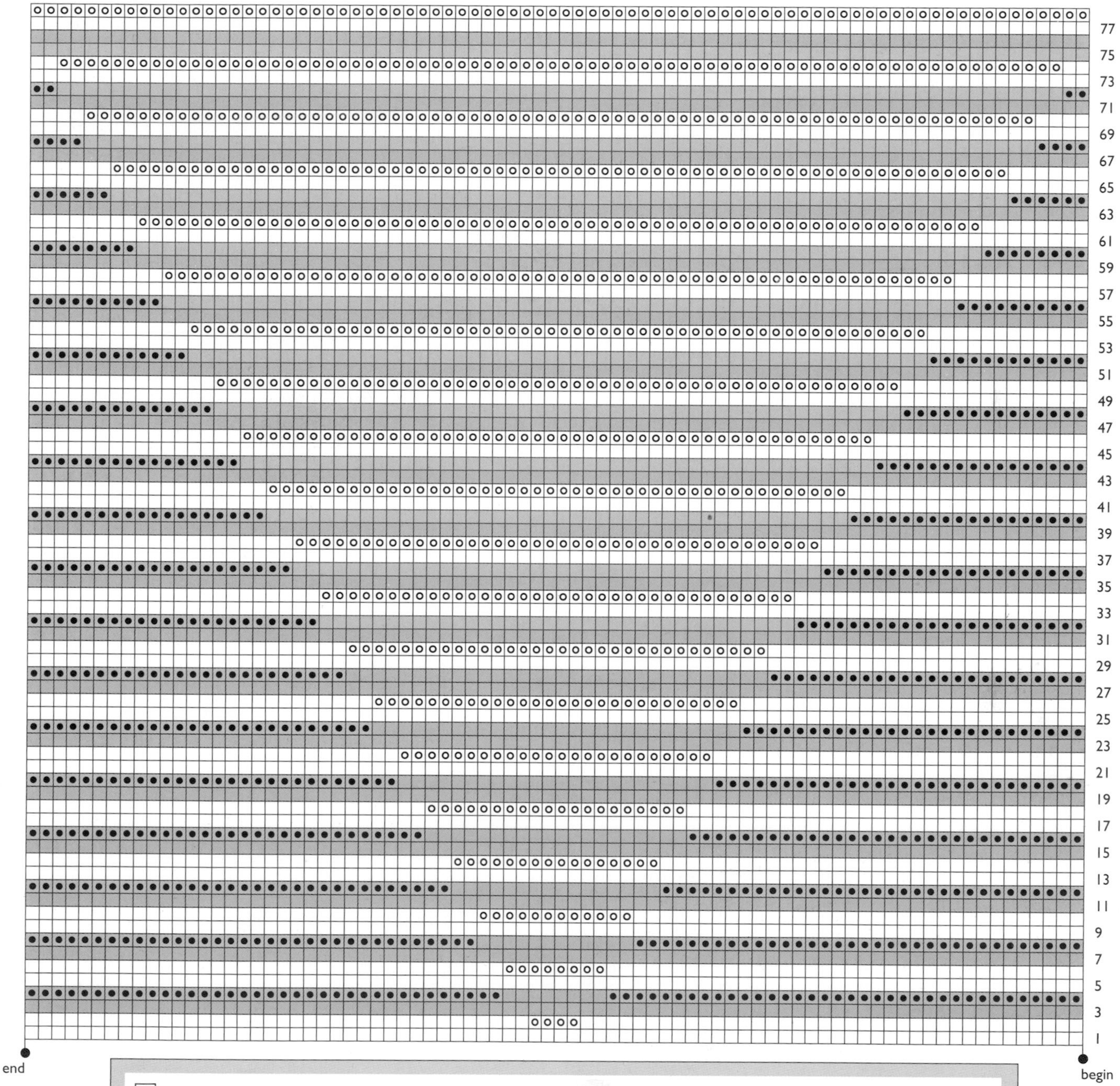

77
75
73
71
69
67
65
63
61
59
57
55
53
51
49
47
45
43
41
39
37
35
33
31
29
27
25
23
21
19
17
15
13
11
9
7
5
3
1

end

begin

	L (light color) yellow-green: knit on RS; purl on WS		D (dark color) dark olive: knit on WS (makes a ridge on RS)
O	L (light color) yellow-green: knit on WS (makes a ridge on RS)	●	stitch marker
	D (dark color) dark olive: knit on RS; purl on WS		

FINISHED SIZE

Hat: 20½"–21¼" (52cm–54 cm) circumference.
Scarf: 9" (23 cm) wide and about 67" (170 cm) long.

YARN

Sport-weight yarn. **Hat** requires about 89 yd (81 m) dark yarn (D) and 62 yd (57 m) light yarn (L). **Scarf** requires about 289 yd (264 m) dark yarn (D) and 310 yd (283 m) light yarn (L). We used Rowan Wool Cotton (50% wool, 50% cotton; 124 yd [113 m]/ 50 g): navy (D), 4 balls, and Noro Silk Garden (45% silk, 45% mohair, 10% lambswool; 110 yd [100 m]/50 g): rainbow (L), 3 balls.

NEEDLES

Hat—US Size 4 (3.5 mm): straight or 16" (40-cm) circular (cir) and set of 4 or 5 double-pointed (dpn). **Scarf**—US Size 4 (3.5 mm): straight. Adjust needle size if necessary to obtain the correct gauge.

NOTIONS

Markers (m); tapestry needle.

GAUGE

Hat brim: 25 sts and 27 rows = 4" (10 cm) in charted pattern. Hat crown: 24 sts and 32 rnds = 4" (10 cm) in St st worked in the rnd with D. Scarf: 25 sts and 27 rows = 4" (10 cm) in charted pattern.

MATCHING HAT AND SCARF

....

This elegant hat-and-scarf set has an easy-to-knit triangular shadow pattern.

NOTES

Before you begin, review Tips—Before You Knit, pages 11–14; Abbreviations, page 134; Techniques, pages 135–140.

The chart for this project is on page 41. It begins with a WS row and does not include the edge stitches. The hat is worked across the first 28 stitches of the chart; the scarf is worked across all 56 stitches.

These projects are worked in diagonal knitting; in order for the stitches to move diagonally, and at the same time keep the side edges straight, one stitch is increased at the beginning of right-side rows and one stitch is decreased at the end of right-side rows. The stitch count remains constant and there are always three edge stitches at each end of the row.

HAT

Brim
With D and straight or cir needle, CO 34 sts.

Row 1: (WS) With D, k3 (3 border sts; not shown on chart), foll chart as indicated for hat, work next 28 sts according to Row 1 of Hat and Scarf chart (page 41), k2, p1 (3 border sts; not shown on chart).

Row 2: (RS) With L, sl 1 kwise, k1, M1 (see Techniques, page 138; these 3 sts form the border), work next 28 sts according to Row 2 of chart, work rem 4 sts as k2tog, k1, p1 (3 border sts; not shown on chart).

Row 3: (WS) With L, sl 1 kwise, k2 (still 3 border sts), work next 28 sts according to Row 3 of chart, k2, p1 (3 border sts).

Row 4: With D, sl 1 kwise, k1, M1, work next 28 sts according to Row 4 of chart, work rem 4 sts as k2tog, k1, p1 (3 border sts).

Row 5: With D, sl 1 kwise, k2 (3 border sts), work next 28 sts according to Row 5 of chart, k2, p1 (3 border sts).

Cont in this manner, inc 1 st after the first 2 sts and dec 1 st before the last 2 sts on every even-numbered row

(see Notes), until Rows 1–28 of chart have been worked on center 28 sts 5 times—piece should measure about 20¾" (52.5 cm) from beg. BO all sts. With yarn threaded on a tapestry needle, sew CO edge to BO edge to form a ring.

Crown

With cir needle, D, and RS facing, pick up and knit 70 sts around the tighter side edge (the edge where each RS row began, and colors were changed) of the brim ring, using the innermost chains (the outside chain will be visible on the RS). Turn brim so WS is facing, place marker (pm), and join into a rnd. Cont in the rnd with RS of crown facing as foll:

Rnd 1: *K2, M1; rep from *—105 sts.
Rnd 2: Knit, inc 3 sts evenly spaced—108 sts.
With D, cont working even in the rnd until crown measures about 5½" (14 cm) from pick-up rnd.

Shape crown

Dec Rnd 1: *K2tog, k14, ssk (see Techniques, page 137); rep from *—96 sts rem.
Knit 2 rnds even.
Dec Rnd 2: *K2tog, k12, ssk; rep from *—84 sts rem.
Knit 2 rnds even.
Dec Rnd 3: *K2tog, k10, ssk; rep from *—72 sts.
Knit 2 rnds even.
Changing to dpn as needed and cont in this manner, dec every third rnd, working 2 fewer sts between decs, until 24 sts rem. *Next rnd:* *K2tog, ssk; rep from *—12 sts rem. *Next rnd:* *K2tog; rep from *—6 sts rem.

FINISHING

Cut yarn, leaving a 4" (10-cm) tail. Thread tail on tapestry needle and draw through rem sts, pull tight, and fasten off on WS. Weave in loose ends. Fold cuff to RS.

SCARF

With D, CO 62 sts.

Bottom border

Row 1: (WS) With D, knit to last st, p1.
Row 2: (RS) Sl 1 kwise, k1, M1 (see Techniques, page 138; these 3 sts form the border), knit to last 4 sts, k2tog, k1, p1 (3 border sts).

Scarf body

Row 1: (WS) Sl 1 kwise, k2 (3 border sts), work next 56 sts according to Row 1 of Hat and Scarf chart (page 41), k2, p1 (3 border sts).
Row 2: (RS) With L, sl 1 kwise, k1, M1 (still 3 border sts), work next 56 sts according to Row 2 of chart, work rem 4 sts as k2tog, k1, p1 (3 border sts).
Row 3: With L, sl 1 kwise, k2 (3 border sts), work next 56 sts according to Row 3 of chart, k2, p1 (3 border sts).
Row 4: With D, sl 1 kwise, k1, M1 (3 border sts), work next 56 sts according to Row 4 of chart, work last 4 sts as k2tog, k1, p1 (3 border sts).
Row 5: With D, sl 1 kwise, k2, work next 56 sts according to Row 5 of chart, k2, p1.
Cont in this manner, inc 1 st after the first 2 sts and dec 1 st before the last 2 sts on every even-numbered row

Hat and Scarf

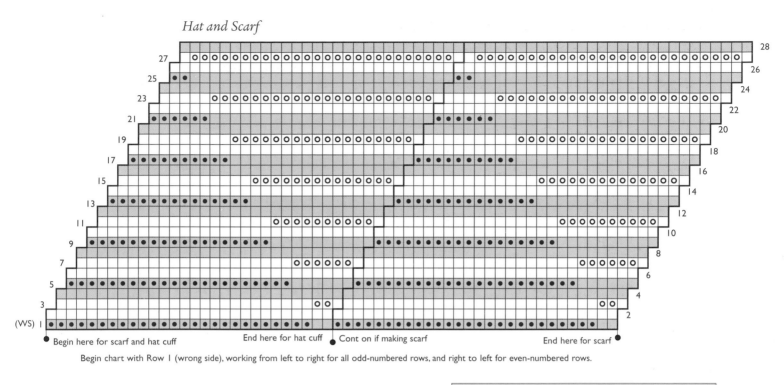

Begin here for scarf and hat cuff   End here for hat cuff   Cont on if making scarf   End here for scarf

Begin chart with Row 1 (wrong side), working from left to right for all odd-numbered rows, and right to left for even-numbered rows.

(see Notes), until Rows 1–28 of chart have been worked on center 56 sts a total of 16 times—piece should measure about 66″ (168 cm) from beg.

Top border
With D, knit 4 rows, maintaining border sts as established.
With D, BO all sts.

FINISHING
Weave in loose ends. Block lightly, if desired.

☐	L (light color): knit on RS; purl on WS
◉	L (light color): knit on WS (makes a ridge on RS)
▨	D (dark color): knit on RS; purl on WS
⊡	D (dark color): knit on WS (makes a ridge on RS)
☐	pattern repeat
●	stitch marker

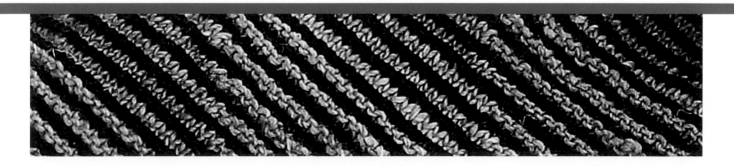

HEART TOP

The body of this top is worked from the bottom up, and the sleeves are knit from the armhole to cuff, which highlights the shadow pattern beautifully. The heart is seen most distinctly by the child (or by an adult) who looks down at it. Such fun!

FINISHED SIZE

28½" (72.5 cm) chest circumference. *Note:* Top will stretch a bit with wear. To fit size 2–4 years.

YARN

Sport-weight yarn. Top requires about 504 yd (460 m) of dark yarn (D) and 252 yd (230 m) each of two light yarns (L1 and L2). We used Rowan Cotton Glacé, (100% cotton; 126 yd [115 m]/50 g): #746 nightshade (D), 4 balls; #747 candy floss (L1) and #802 sunny (L2), 2 balls each.

NEEDLES

US size 2 (2.75 mm): straight. Adjust needle size if necessary to obtain the correct gauge.

NOTIONS

Markers (m); tapestry needle; six ⅝" (1.5-cm) buttons; sharp-point needle and sewing thread to match buttons.

GAUGE

24 sts and 44 rows = 4" (10 cm) in charted pattern.

NOTES

Before beginning, review Tips—Before You Knit, pages 11–14; Abbreviations, page 134; Techniques, pages 135–140.

The charts for this project are on pages 45, 46, and 47. Garter-stitch edge stitches are shown on the body charts; there are no edge stitches for the sleeves.

Stitches for the sleeves are picked up from around the armholes, and the sleeves are worked downward to the cuffs.

BACK

With D, CO 87 sts.

Lower band
With D, knit 7 rows, beg and ending with a WS row.

Body
With RS facing and beg with Row 1, work all sts through Row 74 of Lower Body chart (page 45), working the first 2 sts and last 2 sts of every row in garter st in same color as rest of row (as shown on chart). Change to Upper Body chart (page 46) and work Rows 75–83, working edge sts in garter st as established.

Mark base of armholes
Mark each end of Row 83 to indicate base of armholes. Cont as established through Row 146 of chart (ignore yellow lines indicating front neck shaping).

Back neck and shoulders
With D, knit all sts for 5 rows, ending with a RS row. With WS facing, BO all sts.

FRONT

Work as back through Row 125 of Upper Body chart.

Shape front neck
(WS; Row 126 of chart) Work 37 sts, join new ball of yarn and BO center 13 sts, work to end—37 sts at each side. Working each side separately in patt as established, shape neck as foll (designated by yellow line on chart): At each neck edge, BO 2 sts every other row 3 times—31 sts rem each side. At

each neck edge, dec 1 st every other row 3 times—28 sts rem each side. Work 3 rows even. *Next row:* Dec 1 st at each neck edge—27 sts rem. Cont even through Row 146 of chart.

Shoulder bands

Cont working the two sides separately, with D, knit all sts for 2 rows. *Next row:* (RS) Knit, and *at the same time* work 2 buttonholes as foll: Work 7 sts in pattern, *k2tog, [yo] 2 times, k2tog through back loops (tbl)*, k6, rep from * to *, k6. With WS facing, BO all sts.

Front neckband

(RS) With L2, RS facing, and beg at edge of shoulder band, pick up and knit 52 sts around front neck opening, including both shoulder bands.

Row 1: (WS) With L2, knit to last st, p1.

Row 2: (RS) Change to D, sl 1 kwise, *k2tog, [yo] 2 times, k2tog tbl*, knit to last 5 sts, rep from * to *, p1.

Row 3: Cont with D, sl 1 kwise, knit to last st, *at the same time* dec 4 sts evenly spaced, p1—48 sts rem.

Row 4: Sl 1 kwise, knit to last st, p1.

With WS facing, BO all sts kwise. With sewing needle and thread, sew buttons to back shoulder bands opposite buttonholes. Fasten bands tog by buttoning buttons, overlapping shoulders in preparation for sleeve pick-up.

SLEEVES

With D and RS facing, pick up and knit 77 sts between the armhole markers on back and front, knitting through the doubled layer at the buttoned shoulder bands. *Note:* The pick-up row is Row 1 of Sleeve chart (page 47). Work through Row 8 of chart. *Dec row:* (Row 9 of chart) Dec 1 st each end of needle—2 sts decreased; 75 sts rem. Work 7 rows even. Rep dec row on Row 17. Cont through Row 108 of chart, dec 1 st each end of needle every 8th row in this manner 11 more times—51 sts rem. With D only, cont even until piece measures 9¾" (25 cm) from pick-up row.

Cuff

Join D and knit all sts, dec 1 st each end of needle—49 sts rem. Knit all sts for 6 more rows, ending with a RS row. With WS facing, BO all sts loosely kwise.

FINISHING

With yarn threaded on a tapestry needle and using the mattress st (see Techniques, page 140), sew sleeve and side seams, leaving the lower 2" (5 cm) of side seams open for side vents. Weave in loose ends to WS and secure.

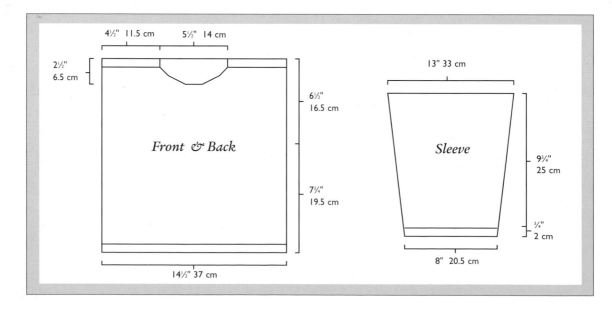

Lower Body

73
71
69
67
65
63
61
59
57
55
53
51
49
47
45
43
41
39
37
35
33
31
29
27
25
23
21
19
17
15
13
11
9
7
5
3
1
end
begin

- L1 (light color 1) #747 candy floss: knit on RS; purl on WS
- O — L1 (light color 1) #747 candy floss: knit on WS (makes a ridge on RS)
- L2 (light color 2) #802 sunny: knit on RS; purl on WS
- + — L2 (light color 2) #802 sunny: knit on WS (makes a ridge on RS)
- D (dark color) #746 nightshade: knit on RS; purl on WS
- ● — D (dark color) #746 nightshade: knit on WS (makes a ridge on RS)
- × — Garter st edges: knit on WS using same color as sts in row

Upper Body

▨ L1 (light color 1) #747 candy floss: knit on RS; purl on WS	⦿ D (dark color) #746 nightshade: knit on WS (makes a ridge on RS)
⊙ L1 (light color 1) #747 candy floss: knit on WS (makes a ridge on RS)	☒ Garter st edges: knit on WS using same color as sts in row
▢ L2 (light color 2) #802 sunny: knit on RS; purl on WS	Front neck shaping
⊞ L2 (light color 2) #802 sunny: knit on WS (makes a ridge on RS)	
▨ D (dark color) #746 nightshade: knit on RS; purl on WS	* mark each end of Row 83 for sleeve placement

Sleeve

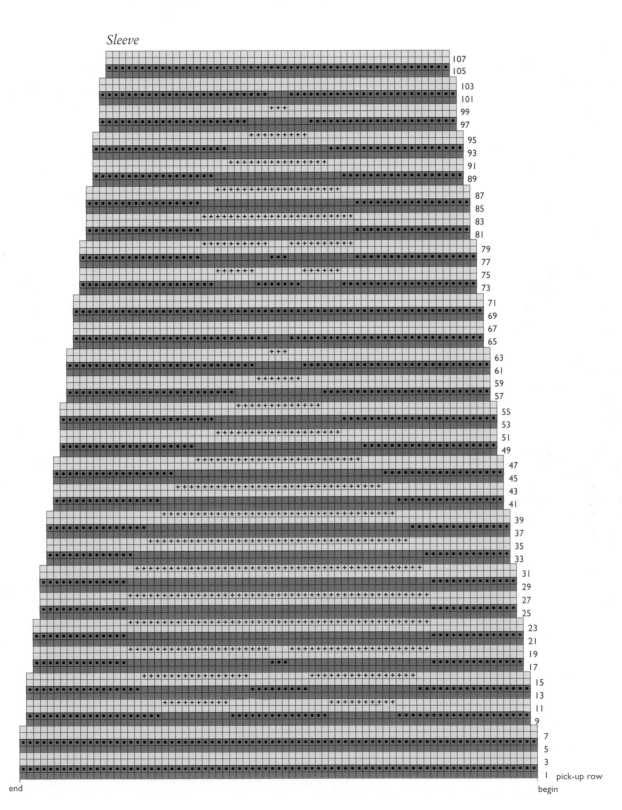

FINISHED SIZE

Small Shawl: 39" (99 cm) wide and 26" (66 cm) long, measured along middle of center back stripe. **Triangles** and **Diagonal Stripes Shawls:** each 54" (137 cm) wide and 38¼" (97 cm) long, measured along middle of center back stripe.

YARN

Fingering-weight yarn. **Small Shawl** requires about 651 yd (595 m) each of dark yarn (D) and light yarn (L), plus 217 yd (199 m) each of two contrasting yarns (CC1 and CC2). **Triangles Shawl** requires about 1085 yd (992 m) each of dark yarn (D) and light yarn (L), plus 434 yd (397 m) each of two contrasting yarns (CC1 and CC2). **Diagonal Stripes Shawl** requires about 1085 yd (992 m) of dark yarn (D), 550 yd (503 m) each of two light yarns (L1 and L2), and 217 yd (199 m) each of two contrasting yarns (CC1 and CC2).

We suggest Harrisville Designs New England Shetland (100% pure virgin wool; 217 yd [198 m]/50 g) in the colors and quantities listed below. **Small Shawl:** #18 aubergine (D) and #07 tundra (L), 2 skeins each; #65 poppy (CC1) and #35 chianti (CC2), 1 skein each. **Triangles Shawl:** #85 ebony (D) and #45 pearl (L), 5 skeins each; #81 mustard (CC 1) and #80 foliage (CC 2), 1 skein each.

WING SHAWLS

·················

Elegant shawls drape your body naturally and don't fall off when you move. The wing shawl may be knitted in a combination of sizes and patterns. Three variations are given: a small shawl, and a large shawl in two different shadow patterns. The small shawl could be worn over a dress at an evening party. The larger-size shawls are comfortable and cozy—perfect for everyday life.

NOTES

Before beginning, review Tips—Before You Knit, pages 11–14; Abbreviations, page 134; Techniques, pages 135–140.

The charts for the Small Shawl are on page 51. The charts for the Triangles shawl are on pages 52 and 54. The charts for the Diagonal Stripes Shawl are on pages 58, 59, 62, and 63. All charts include border stitches; the shadow patterns are enclosed in red lines that denote the pattern repeat frames.

A schematic for this project is on page 50. Each shawl is worked back and forth on a circular needle (to accommodate the large number of stitches) from the left side to the right side. Each shawl begins with a contrast-color band worked in garter stitch (left side stripe), followed by a shadow pattern for the left side of the shawl, a broad garter-stitch stripe at the center, another shadow pattern for the right side, and ends with a contrast-color garter-stitch band (right side stripe).

The general instructions for the shawl components are given first (General Instructions), followed by the instructions for the specific shawls.

The yarns for each of these shawls can be purchased in kit form; see Resources, page 142 for more information.

GENERAL INSTRUCTIONS

LEFT SIDE STRIPE: (worked in CC1)
CO required number of sts for shawl of your choice. Cont as foll:
Row 1: (WS) Knit to last st, p1.
Row 2: (RS) Sl 1 kwise, k1f&b, knit to last 3 sts, k2tog, p1.
Row 3: (WS) Sl 1 kwise, knit to last st, p1.
Repeat Rows 2 and 3 six more times, ending with a WS row—15 rows total; 8 garter ridges on RS; piece should measure about

Small Shawl

Diagonal Stripes Shawl: #36 garnet (D), 5 skeins; #35 chianti (L1) and #65 poppy (L2), 3 skeins each; #87 brass (CC1) and #82 straw (CC2), 1 skein each.

NEEDLES

US Size 2 (2.75 mm): 32" (80-cm) circular (cir). Adjust needle size if necessary to obtain the correct gauge.

NOTIONS

Markers (m); tapestry needle.

GAUGE

24 sts and 46 rows = 4" (10 cm) in charted pattern.

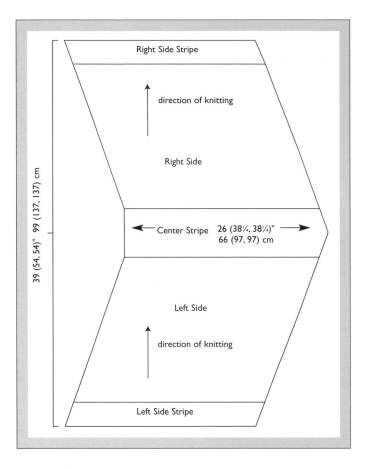

Right Side Stripe

direction of knitting

Right Side

← Center Stripe 26 (38¼, 38¼)" →
66 (97, 97) cm

39 (54, 54)" 99 (137, 137) cm

Left Side

direction of knitting

Left Side Stripe

Row 17: (RS) Join CC1, sl 1 kwise, knit to last st, p1.

Row 18: (WS) Sl 1 kwise, knit to last st, p1.

Row 19: (RS) With CC2, sl 1 kwise, knit to last st, p1.

Row 20: (WS) Sl 1 kwise, knit to last st, p1.

Cut off CC2, leaving a 4″ (10-cm) tail.

Center Stripe, Right Side (worked in CC1)

Note: This part of the center stripe is worked straight at the neck edge and slants upward at the lower edge.

Row 21: (RS) Join CC1, sl 1 kwise, ssk (see Techniques, page 137), knit to last st, p1—1 st decreased.

Row 22: (WS) Sl 1 kwise, knit to last st, p1.

Rep Rows 21 and 22 seven more times—16 rows total; 8 garter ridges on RS; 8 sts decreased total. Cont as specified for the shawl of your choice.

RIGHT SIDE STRIPE (worked in CC2)

Row 1: (RS) With CC2, sl 1 kwise, ssk, knit to last 2 sts, k1f&b, p1.

Row 2: (WS) Sl 1 kwise, knit to last st, p1.

Rep Rows 1 and 2 six more times, then work Row 1 again—15 rows total; 7 garter ridges on RS; stripe should measure about 1¼″ (3.2 cm) from beg. With WS facing, BO all sts kwise to form 8th ridge on RS. Cut yarn, leaving 4″ (10-cm) tails.

SMALL SHAWL

Left Side Stripe

With CC1, and using the knitted method (see Techniques, page 136), CO 150 sts. Work according to general instructions, beginning on page 48.

Left Side

(worked with light ridges on a dark background; see Basic Pattern 1 on page 7) Join D and work Small Shawl, Left Side chart (page 51) as foll:

Row 1 and all RS rows with D: (RS) With D, sl 1 kwise, k1f&b, knit to last 3 sts, k2tog, p1.

Row 2: (WS) With D, sl 1 kwise, k7 (8 border sts), p134, k7, p1 (8 border sts).

1¼″ (3.2 cm) from beg. Cut yarn, leaving 4″ (10-cm) tails. Cont as specified for the shawl of your choice.

CENTER STRIPE

Center Stripe, Left Side (worked in CC2)

Note: This part of the center stripe is worked straight at the neck edge and slants downward at the lower edge.

Row 1: (RS) Join CC2, sl 1 kwise, k1f&b, knit to last st, p1—1 st increased.

Row 2: (WS) Sl 1 kwise, knit to last st, p1.

Rep Rows 1 and 2 seven more times—16 rows total; 8 garter ridges on RS; 8 sts increased total. Do not cut yarn.

Center Stripe, Center Rows (worked in CC1 and CC2)

Note: This part of the center stripe is worked straight at both edges.

Row 3 and all RS rows with L: (RS) With L, sl 1 kwise, k1f&b, knit to last 3 sts, k2tog, p1.

Row 4: (WS) With L, sl 1 kwise, k7 (8 border sts), sl m, k134 (forms a L ridge on RS), sl m, k7, p1 (8 border sts).

Cont working these 4 rows until a total of 196 rows have been worked—49 garter ridges in L. With D, work Rows 1 and 2 once more—198 rows total; piece should measure about 17¼" (44 cm) from beg of charted patt (not including left side stripe).

Center Stripe

With CC1, work according to general instructions (page 50).

Right Side

(worked with dark ridges on a light background; see Basic Pattern 2 on page 7) Join L and work Small Shawl, Right Side chart as foll:

Row 1 and all RS rows with L: (RS) With L, sl 1 kwise, ssk, knit to last 2 sts, k1f&b, p1.

Row 2: (WS) Sl 1 kwise, k7, sl m, p134, sl m, k7, p1.

Row 3 and all RS rows with D: (RS) With D, sl 1 kwise, ssk, knit to last 2 sts, k1f&b, p1.

Row 4: (WS) Sl 1 kwise, k7, k134, k7, p1.

Cont working these 4 rows until a total of 196 rows have been worked—49 garter ridges in D. With L, work Rows 1 and 2 once more—198 rows total.

Right Side Stripe

With CC2, work according to general instructions (page 50).

FINISHING

Weave in all ends to WS. Block to measurements (see schematic, page 50).

V		Slip 1 st kwise
∖		Ssk
∕		K2tog
⸜⸝		K1f&b
·		Purl on RS in whatever color is shown (edge st)
		LI: knit on RS; purl on WS
O		LI: knit on WS
▧		D: knit on RS; purl on WS
⬤		D: knit on WS
		pattern repeat
|		boundary between body and border sts

Small Shawl, Right Side

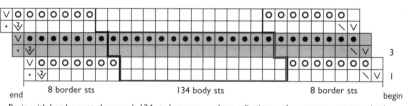

end   8 border sts   134 body sts   8 border sts   begin

Begin with border patt, then work 134 sts between markers, *adjusting markers as necessary to maintain 134 sts between them.* Work patt Rows 1–4 a total of 49 times, then work 2 rows L as shown—198 rows total.

Small Shawl, Left Side

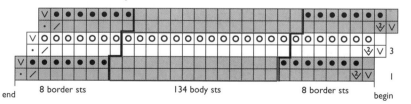

end   8 border sts   134 body sts   8 border sts   begin

Begin with border patt, then work 134 sts between markers, *adjusting markers as necessary to maintain 134 sts between them.* Work patt Rows 1–4 a total of 49 times, then work 2 rows D as shown—198 rows total.

TRIANGLES SHAWL

The basic patterns in this shawl form two large triangles on each side of the shawl. The boundary between light and dark will lie along the shoulder.

Left Side Stripe

With CC1 and using the knitted method (see Techniques, page 136), CO 225 sts. Work according to general instructions (page 48).

Left Side

(worked with light ridges on a dark background that give way to dark ridges on a light background; see Basic Patterns 1 and 2 on page 7) Join D and work Triangles Shawl, Left Side chart (below) as foll:

Row 1 and all RS rows in D: (RS) With D, sl 1 kwise, k1f&b, knit to last 3 sts, k2tog, p1.

Row 2: (WS) With D, sl 1 kwise, k7 (8 border sts), p209, k7, p1 (8 border sts).

Row 3 and all RS rows in L: (RS) With L, sl 1 kwise, k1f&b, knit to last 3 sts, k2tog, p1.

Row 4: (WS) With L, sl 1 kwise, k7, k208, p1, k7, p1.

Row 6: (WS) With D, sl 1 kwise, k7, p207, k2, k7, p1.

Row 8: (WS) With L, sl 1 kwise, k7, k205, p4, k7, p1.

Row 10: (WS) With D, sl 1 kwise, k7, p204, k5, k7, p1.

V	Slip 1 st kwise
/	K2tog
ⱱ	K1f&b
·	Purl on RS in whatever color is shown (edge st)
□	L1: knit on RS; purl on WS
⊙	L1: knit on WS
▨	D: knit on RS; purl on WS
⬤	D: knit on WS
I	boundary between body and border sts

Triangles Shawl, Left Side

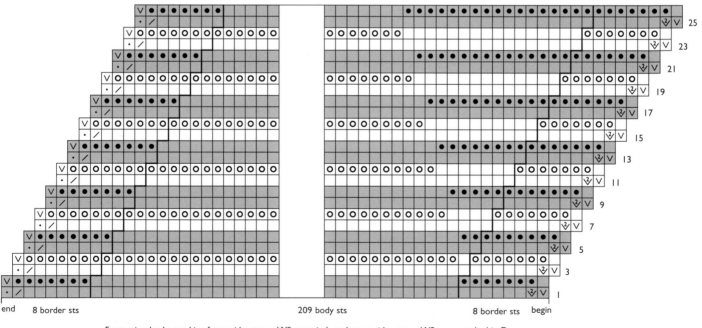

end   8 border sts   209 body sts   8 border sts   begin

Form triangles by working fewer ridge sts on WS rows in L, and more ridge sts on WS rows worked in D.

Triangles Shawl

Row 12: (WS) With L, sl 1 kwise, k7, k202, p7, k7, p1.

Row 14: (WS) With D, sl 1 kwise, k7, p201, k8, k7, p1.

Row 16: (WS) With L, sl 1 kwise, k7, k199, p10, k7, p1.

Row 18: (WS) With D, sl 1 kwise, k7, p198, k11, k7, p1.

Row 20: (WS) With L, sl 1 kwise, k7, k196, p13, k7, p1.

Row 22: (WS) With D, sl 1 kwise, k7, p195, k14, k7, p1.

Row 24: (WS) With L, sl 1 kwise, k7, k193, p16, k7, p1.

Row 26: (WS) With D, sl 1 kwise, k7, p192, k17, k7, p1.

Cont in this manner, working 8 border sts at each edge every row and knitting all patt sts on WS rows, and *at the same time* shifting the shadow patt every WS row worked in D by purling 3 fewer sts and knitting 3 more sts, and shifting the shadow patt every WS row worked in L by knitting 3 fewer sts and purling 3 more sts, until 278 rows of patt have been worked. Work last 4 rows as foll:

Row 279: (RS) With L, sl 1 kwise, k1f&b, knit to last 3 sts, k2tog, p1.

Row 280: (WS) With L, sl 1 kwise, k7, k1, p208, k7, p1.

Row 281: (RS) With D, sl 1 kwise, k1f&b, knit to last 3 sts, k2tog, p1.

Row 282: (WS) With D, sl 1 kwise, k7, p209, k7, p1—piece should measure about 25¾" (65.5 cm) from CO edge (including left side stripe).

Center Stripe

With CC1, work according to general instructions (page 50).

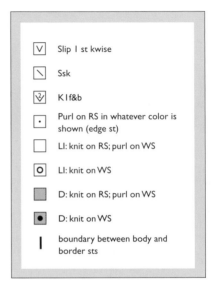

V	Slip 1 st kwise
\	Ssk
ⱱ	K 1f&b
·	Purl on RS in whatever color is shown (edge st)
☐	Ll: knit on RS; purl on WS
○	Ll: knit on WS
▨	D: knit on RS; purl on WS
▨•	D: knit on WS
|	boundary between body and border sts

Triangles Shawl, Right Side

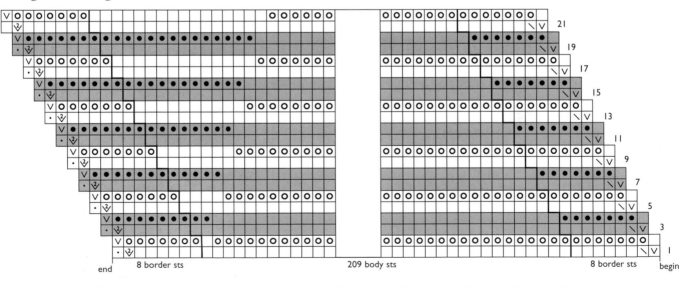

end   8 border sts   209 body sts   8 border sts   begin

Form triangles by working fewer ridge sts on WS rows worked in L, and more ridge sts on WS rows worked in D.

Right Side

(worked with light ridges on a dark background that give way to dark ridges on a light background in the opposite direction as the left side) Join L and work Triangles Shawl, Right Side chart (page 54) as foll:

Row 1 and all RS rows in L: (RS) With L, sl 1 kwise, ssk, knit to last 2 sts, k1f&b, p1.

Row 2: (WS) With L, sl 1 kwise, k7 (8 border sts), p1, k208, k7, p1 (8 border sts).

Row 3 and all RS rows in D: (RS) With D, sl 1 kwise, ssk, knit to last 2 sts, k1f&b, p1.

Row 4: (WS) With D, sl 1 kwise, k7, k2, p207, k7, p1.

Row 6: (WS) With L, sl 1 kwise, k7, p4, k205, k7, p1.

Row 8: (WS) With D, sl 1 kwise, k7, k5, p204, k7, p1.

Row 10: (WS) With L, sl 1 kwise, k7, p7, k202, k7, p1.

Row 12: (WS) With D, sl 1 kwise, k7, k8, p201, k7, p1.

Cont in this manner, working 8 border sts at each edge every row and knitting all patt sts on WS rows, and *at the same time* shifting the shadow patt every WS row worked in D by knitting 3 more sts and purling 3 fewer sts, and shifting the shadow patt every WS row worked in L by purling 3 more sts and knitting 3 fewer sts, until 274 rows of patt have been worked. Work last 8 rows as foll:

Row 275: (RS) With D, sl 1 kwise, ssk, knit to last 2 sts, k1f&b, p1.

Row 276: (WS) With D, sl 1 kwise, k7 (8 border sts), k205, p4, k7, p1 (8 border sts).

Row 277: (RS) With L, sl 1 kwise, ssk, knit to last 2 sts, k1f&b, p1.

Row 278: (WS) With L, sl 1 kwise, k7, p208, k1, k7, p1.

Row 279: (RS) With D, sl 1 kwise, ssk, knit to last 2 sts, k1f&b, p1.

Row 280: (WS) With D, sl 1 kwise, k7, k208, p1, k7, p1.

Row 281: (RS) With L, sl 1 kwise, ssk, knit to last 2 sts, k1f&b, p1.

Row 282: (WS) With L, sl 1 kwise, k7, p209, k7, p1.

Right Side Stripe

With CC2, work according to general instructions (page 50).

DIAGONAL STRIPES SHAWL

Left Side Stripe

With CC1 and using the knitted method (see Techniques, page 136), CO 219 sts. Work according to general instructions (page 48).

Left Side

(worked in D and L1 in diagonal stripes that shift to the left when viewed from the RS) Join D and work Large Diagonal Stripes Shawl, Left Side chart (pages 58 and 59; note that large size of chart necessitates abbreviating the chart to illustrate only partial areas of the foll text rows) as foll:

Row 1 and all RS rows worked in D: (RS) Sl 1 kwise, k1f&b, knit to last 3 sts, k2tog, p1.

Row 2: (WS) With D, sl 1 kwise, k7 (8 border sts), [p19, k18] 5 times, p18, k7, p1 (8 border sts).

Row 3 and all RS rows worked in L1: (RS) With L1, sl 1 kwise, k1f&b, knit to last 3 sts, k2tog, p1.

Row 4: (WS) With L1, sl 1 kwise, k7, k17, [p19, k18] 5 times, p1, k7, p1.

Row 6: (WS) With D, sl 1 kwise, k7, p16, [k18, p19] 5 times, k2, k7, p1.

Row 8: (WS) With L1, sl 1 kwise, k7, k14, [p19, k18] 5 times, p4, k7, p1.

Row 10: (WS) With D, sl 1 kwise, k7, p13, [k18, p19] 5 times, k5, k7, p1.

Row 12: (WS) With L1, sl 1 kwise, k7, k11, [p19, k18] 5 times, p7, k7, p1.

Row 14: (WS) With D, sl 1 kwise, k7, p10, [k18, p19] 5 times, k8, k7, p1.

Row 16: (WS) With L1, sl 1 kwise, k7, k8, [p19, k18] 5 times, p10, k7, p1.

Row 18: (WS) With D, sl 1 kwise, k7, p7, [k18, p19] 5 times, k11, k7, p1.

Row 20: (WS) With L1, sl 1 kwise, k7, k5, [p19, k18] 5 times, p13, k7, p1.

Row 22: (WS) With D, sl 1 kwise, k7, p4, [k18, p19] 5 times, k14, k7, p1.

Row 24: (WS) With L1, sl 1 kwise, k7, k2, [p19, k18] 5 times, p16, k7, p1.

Row 26: (WS) With D, sl 1 kwise, k7, p1, [k18, p19] 5 times, k17, k7, p1.

Row 28: (WS) With L1, sl 1 kwise, k7, p18, [k18, p19] 5 times, k7, p1.

Row 30: (WS) With D, sl 1 kwise, k7, k16, [p19, k18] 5 times, p2, k7, p1.

Row 32: (WS) With L1, sl 1 kwise, k7, p15, [k18, p19] 5 times, k3, k7, p1.

Row 34: (WS) With D, sl 1 kwise, k7, k13, [p19, k18] 5 times, p5, k7, p1.

Row 36: (WS) With L1, sl 1 kwise, k7, p12, [k18, p19] 5 times, k6, k7, p1.

Row 38: (WS) With D, sl 1 kwise, k7, k10, [p19, k18] 5 times, p8, k7, p1.

Row 40: (WS) With L1, sl 1 kwise, k7, p9, [k18, p19] 5 times, k9, k7, p1.

Cont in this manner, working 8 border sts at each edge every row and knitting all patt sts on WS rows, and *at the same time* shifting the diagonal stripes patt 3 sts to the left (as viewed from the RS) every WS row. For example, on WS Row 36 with L1, work p12 after the first 8 border sts. On the next L1 WS row (Row 40), p9 after the first 8 border sts (3 fewer purl sts than on Row 36). This 3-st shift sets up the patt for the rest of the row. For example, on WS Row 34 with D, k13 after the first 8 border sts. On the next D WS row (Row 38), k10 after the first 8 border sts

Diagonal Stripes Shawl

Diagonal Stripes Shawl, Left Side

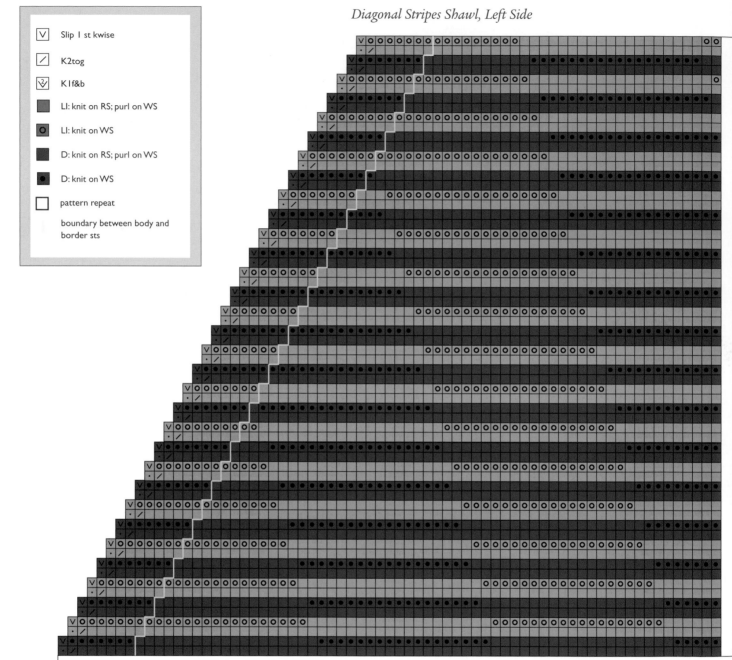

	Slip 1 st kwise
	K2tog
	K1f&b
	LI: knit on RS; purl on WS
	LI: knit on WS
	D: knit on RS; purl on WS
	D: knit on WS
	pattern repeat
	boundary between body and border sts

end | 8 border sts | 203 body sts; work 280 rows as established

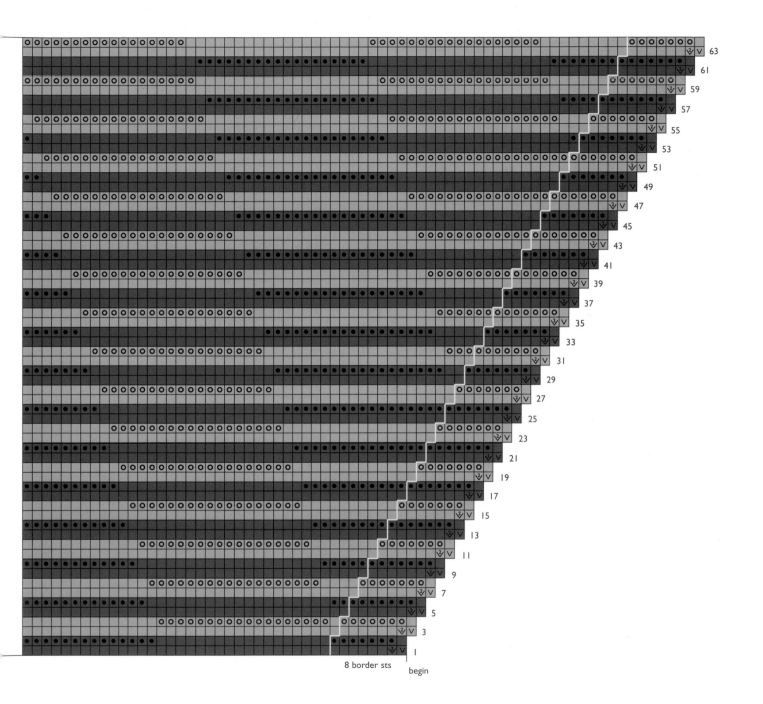

63
61
59
57
55
53
51
49
47
45
43
41
39
37
35
33
31
29
27
25
23
21
19
17
15
13
11
9
7
5
3
1

8 border sts   begin

(3 fewer knit sts than on Row 34). Use the rows detailed below to help you keep track of the pattern.

Row 50: (WS) With D, sl 1 kwise, k7, k1, [p19, k18] 5 times, p17, k7, p1.

Row 100: (WS) With L1, sl 1 kwise, k7, p1, [k18, p19] 5 times, k17, k7, p1.

Row 150: (WS) With D, sl 1 kwise, k7, [p19, k18] 5 times, p18, k7, p1.

Row 200: (WS) With L1, sl 1 kwise, k7, [k18, p19] 5 times, k18, k7, p1.

Row 250: (WS) With D, sl 1 kwise, k7, p18, [k18, p19] 5 times, k7, p1.

Row 280: (WS; final row) With L1, sl 1 kwise, k7, p14, [k18, p19] 5 times, k4, k7, p1.

When Row 280 has been completed, piece should measure about 25¾" (65.5 cm) from CO edge.

Center Stripe

With CC1, work according to general instructions (page 50).

Right Side

(worked in D and L2 in diagonal stripes that shift to the right when viewed from the RS) Join D and work Diagonal Stripes Shawl, Right Side chart (pages 62 and 63; note that large size of chart necessitates abbreviating the chart to illustrate only partial areas of the foll text rows) as foll:

Row 1 and all other RS rows in D: Sl 1 kwise, ssk, knit to last 2 sts, k1f&b, p1. There are 8 border sts at each edge and 203 pattern sts in the center.

Row 2: (WS) With D, sl 1 kwise, k7 (8 border sts), p14, [k18, p19] 5 times, k4, k7, p1 (8 border sts).

Row 3 and all other RS rows in L2: Sl 1 kwise, ssk, knit to last 2 sts, k1f&b, p1.

Row 4: (WS) With L2, sl 1 kwise, k7, k15, [p19, k18] 5 times, p3, k7, p1.

Row 6: (WS) With D, sl 1 kwise, k7, p17, [k18, p19] 5 times, k1, k7, p1.

Row 8: (WS) With L2, sl 1 kwise, k7, [k18, p19] 5 times, k18, k7, p1.

Row 10: (WS) With D, sl 1 kwise, k7, k1, [p19, k18] 5 times, p17, k7, p1.

Row 12: (WS) With L2, sl 1 kwise, k7, p3, [k18, p19] 5 times, k15, k7, p1.

Row 14: (WS) With D, sl 1 kwise, k7, k4, [p19, k18] 5 times, p14, k7, p1.

Row 16: (WS) With L2, sl 1 kwise, k7, p6, [k18, p19] 5 times, k12, k7, p1.

Row 18: (WS) With D, sl 1 kwise, k7, k7, [p19, k18] 5 times, p11, k7, p1.

Row 20: (WS) With L2, sl 1 kwise, k7, p9, [k18, p19] 5 times, k9, k7, p1.

Row 22: (WS) With D, sl 1 kwise, k7, k10, [p19, k18] 5 times, p8, k7, p1.

Row 24: (WS) With L2, sl 1 kwise, k7, p12, [k18, p19] 5 times, k6, k7, p1.

Row 26: (WS) With D, sl 1 kwise, k7, k13, [p19, k18] 5 times, p5, k7, p1.

Row 28: (WS) With L2, sl 1 kwise, k7, p15, [k18, p19] 5 times, k3, k7, p1.

Row 30: (WS) With D, sl 1 kwise, k7, k16, [p19, k18] 5 times, p2, k7, p1.

Row 32: (WS) With L2, sl 1 kwise, k7, p18, [k18, p19] 5 times, k7, p1.

Row 34: (WS) With D, sl 1 kwise, k7, p1, [k18, p19] 5 times, k17, k7, p1.

Row 36: (WS) With L2, sl 1 kwise, k7, k2, [p19, k18] 5 times, p16, k7, p1.

Row 38: (WS) With D, sl 1 kwise, k7, p4, [k18, p19] 5 times, k14, k7, p1.

Row 40: (WS) With L2, sl 1 kwise, k7, k5, [p19, k18] 5 times, p13, k7, p1.

Row 42: (WS) With D, sl 1 kwise, k7, p7, [k18, p19] 5 times, k11, k7, p1.

Row 44: (WS) With L2, sl 1 kwise, k7, k8, [p19, k18] 5 times, p10, k7, p1.

Row 46: (WS) With D, sl 1 kwise, k7, p10, [k18, p19] 5 times, k8, k7, p1.

Row 48: (WS) With L2, sl 1 kwise, k7, k11, [p19, k18] 5 times, p6, k7, p1.

Row 50: (WS) With D, sl 1 kwise, k7, p13, [k18, p19] 5 times, k5, k7, p1.

Cont in this manner, working 8 border sts at each edge every row and knitting all patt sts on WS rows, and *at the same time* shifting the diagonal stripes patt 3 sts to the right (as viewed from the RS) every WS row. For example, on WS Row 44 with L2, k8 after the first 8 border sts. On the next L2 WS row (Row 48), k11 after the first 8 border sts (3 more knit sts than on Row 44). Use the rows detailed below to help you keep track of the pattern.

Row 100: (WS) With L, sl 1 kwise, k7, k13, [p19, k18] 5 times, p5, k7, p1.

Row 150: (WS) With D, sl 1 kwise, k7, p8, [k18, p19] 5 times, k10, k7, p1.

Cont in this manner until a total of 280 rows have been worked, ending by working the last 2 rows in L2.

Right Edge Stripe

With CC2, work according to general instructions (page 50).

FINISHING

Weave in loose ends. Block to measurements (see schematic on page 50).

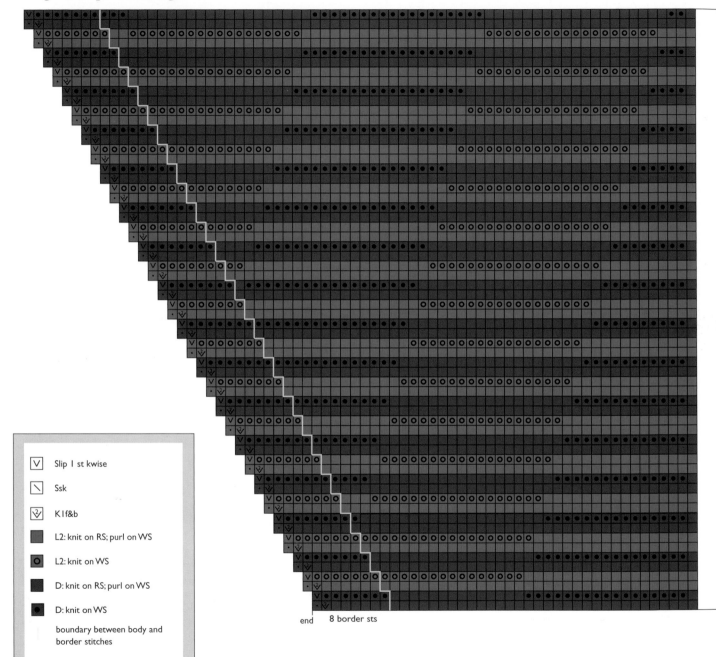

Slip I st kwise

Ssk

K I f&b

L2: knit on RS; purl on WS

L2: knit on WS

D: knit on RS; purl on WS

D: knit on WS

boundary between body and
border stitches

end   8 border sts

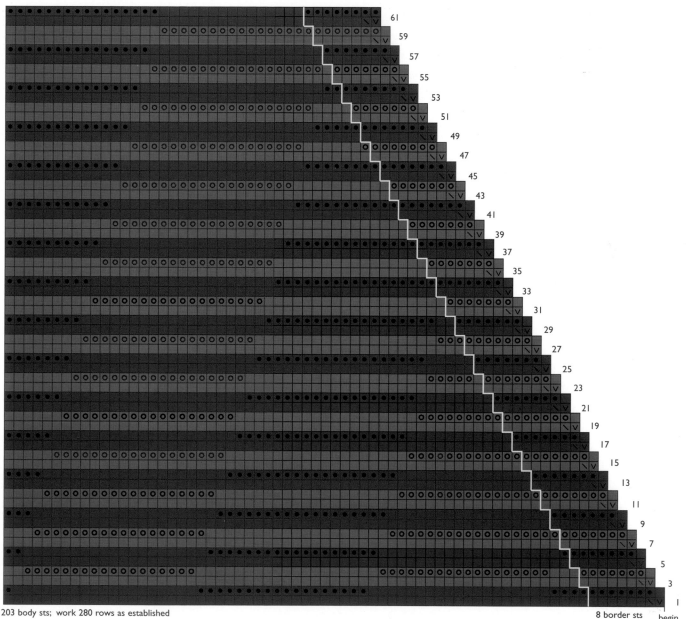

61
59
57
55
53
51
49
47
45
43
41
39
37
35
33
31
29
27
25
23
21
19
17
15
13
11
9
7
5
3
1

203 body sts; work 280 rows as established

8 border sts   begin

FINISHED SIZE

30½ (32, 33½)" (77.5 [81.5, 85] cm) chest circumference. To fit size 4 (6, 8) years. Sweater shown measures 30½" (77.5 cm).

YARN

DK-weight yarn. Sweater requires about 375 (500, 625) yd (343 [457, 572] m) of dark yarn (D) and 375 (500, 500) yd (343 [457, 457] m) of light yarn (L). We used Rowan Wool Cotton (50% wool, 50% cotton; 125 yd [113 m]/50 g): #909 French navy (D), 3 (4, 5) balls; #953 August (L), 3 (4, 4) balls.

NEEDLES

Body and sleeves—Size 2 (3 mm): straight. Edging—Sizes 1 (2.5 mm) and 2 (3 mm): 16" (40-cm) circular (cir). Adjust needle size if necessary to obtain the correct gauge.

NOTIONS

About 2–3 yd (1.8–2.7 m) smooth cotton waste yarn in a contrasting color for provisional CO and stitch holders; markers (m); tapestry needle; long sewing pins.

GAUGE

25 sts and 44 rows = 4" (10 cm) in Basic Pattern 2 on size 2 (3 mm) needles.

SQUARED TOP

Although it may look complex, this child's sweater is really quite easy to knit. The front and back are essentially two large squares, each featuring a block of Basic Pattern 1 (light ridges on a dark background) embedded within the main pattern of Basic Pattern 2 (dark ridges on a light background). The sleeves are worked using the same patterns, with the smaller square block pattern positioned on the upper sleeve.

NOTES

Before beginning, review Tips—Before You Knit, pages 11–14; Abbreviations, page 134; Techniques, pages 135–140.

The main body of the sweater is worked with dark ridges against a light background (Basic Pattern 2 on page 7). The contrasting center block is worked with light ridges against a dark background (Basic Pattern 1 on page 7).

The charts for this sweater are on pages 68 and 69. Edge stitches are not shown on the charts.

A schematic for this project is on page 66. The front and back are worked from side to side, beginning with a provisional (temporary) CO. The sleeves are worked from shoulder to cuff starting with stitches picked up from the upper body.

The sides of the sweater are grafted together with Kitchener stitch for an almost seamless appearance.

Instructions are given for the smallest size with the larger sizes in parentheses. If there is only one number, it applies to all sizes.

STITCH GUIDE

Lower Edge Border: (worked on 8 sts in garter st)

RS rows: Sl 1 kwise, k7, work as instructed to end of row.

WS rows: Work in pattern as instructed to last 8 sts, k7, p1.

Edge Stitches: Excluding the front and back set-up rows, work 1 edge st at each end of row as folls: sl 1 kwise at beg of row, p1 at end of row. On the set-up row, work all sts as given in instructions.

FRONT

Right Side

With larger straight needles, waste yarn, and using the knitted method (see Techniques, page 136), temporarily CO 96 (100, 112) sts. (This temporary CO will be removed later.) Join L and work Body chart (page 68) across 88 (92, 104) sts, and lower edge border across 8 sts as foll:

Set-up row: (WS) With L, p88 (92, 104), place marker (pm), k7, p1 (8 border sts). This row will later be grafted together with a single L row of the back to form a stripe of L at the side edge.

Row 1: (RS) With D, sl 1 kwise, k7, slip marker (sl m), k87 (91, 103), p1.

Row 2: (WS) With D, sl 1 kwise, k87 (91, 103), sl m, k7, p1.

Row 3: With L, sl 1 kwise, k7, sl m, k87 (91, 103), p1.

Row 4: With L, sl 1 kwise, p87 (91, 103), sl m, k7, p1.

Rep Rows 1–4 until there are a total of 38 (38, 42) pattern rows (excluding set-up row), ending with 2 rows of D. Cont working first 26 (26, 34) sts and last 24 sts as established, beg with Row 1, work Block Pattern chart (page 68) on center 46 (50, 54) sts as foll:

Row 39 (39, 43): (RS) With L, sl 1 kwise, k7, sl m, k18 (18, 26), pm, k46 (50, 54), pm, k23, p1.

Row 40 (40, 44): (WS) With L, sl 1 kwise, p23, sl m, k46 (50, 54), sl m, p18 (18, 26), sl m, k7, p1.

Row 41 (41, 45): (RS) With D, sl 1 kwise, k7, sl m, knit to last st, p1.

Row 42 (42, 46): (WS) Sl 1 kwise, k23, sl m, p46 (50, 54), sl m, k18 (18, 26), sl m, k7, p1.

Rep the last 4 rows 1 (2, 2) more time(s)—46 (50, 54) rows total, excluding set-up row.

Shape neck

Beg Front Neck chart (page 68) with RS Row 47 (51, 55) in L, working lower 8 sts in garter-st border, 18 (18, 26) sts according to Body chart (Basic Pattern 2), 46 (50, 54) sts according to Block Pattern chart (Basic Pattern 1), and rem 24 sts according to Body chart (Basic Pattern 2). *Note:* Only 16 sts of block patt are shown due to chart size limitations; rep the sts shown as necessary to complete the 46 (50, 54)-st block patt. *Next row:* (WS Row 48 [52, 56] of chart) BO 4 sts, work to end—92 (96, 108) sts rem. Cont in

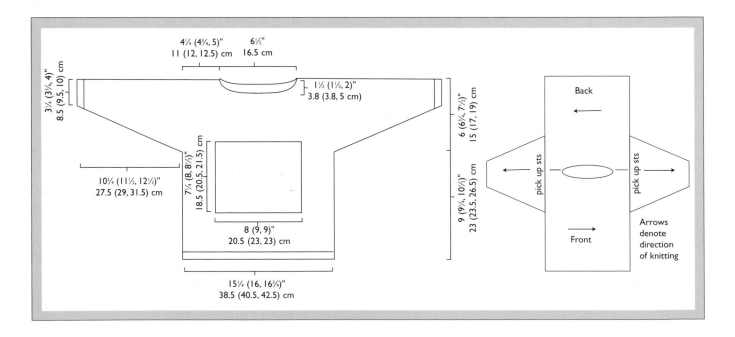

patt, BO 2 sts at beg of next 1 (1, 2) WS row(s)—90 (94, 104) sts rem. Cont in patt, dec 1 st (k2tog) at beg of next 3 WS rows—87 (91, 101) sts rem. Work 3 rows even in patt. *Next row:* (WS Row 60 [64, 70] of chart) Dec 1 st, work to end of row—86 (90, 100) sts rem. Work even in patt for 46 (46, 42) rows. *Next row:* (RS Row 107 [111, 113] of chart) Work in patt to last 2 sts, k1f&b, p1—87 (91, 101) sts. Work 3 rows even in patt. Inc 1 st in this manner at the end of next 3 RS rows—90 (94, 104) sts. Using the backward loop method (see Techniques, page 135), CO 2 sts at the end of next 1 (1, 2) RS row(s)—92 (96, 108) sts. CO 4 sts in this manner at the end of next RS row (Row 119 [123, 127] of chart)—96 (100, 112) sts. Work Row 120 (124, 128) to complete neck.

Left side

Cont as foll:

Row 121 (125, 129): (RS) With D, sl 1 kwise, k7, sl m, knit to last st, p1.

Row 122 (126, 130): (WS) Sl 1 kwise, k23, sl m, p46 (50, 54), sl m, k18 (18, 26), sl m, k7, p1.

Row 123 (127, 131): With L, sl 1 kwise, k7, sl m, knit to last st, p1.

Row 124 (128, 132): Sl 1 kwise, p23, k46 (50, 54), sl m, p18 (18, 26), sl m, k7, p1.

Rep the last 4 rows 1 (2, 2) more time(s) to complete block patt. Remove markers on each side of block patt. Maintaining 8 border sts as established, work all rem sts according to Body chart as foll:

Row 129 (137, 141): (RS) With D, sl 1 kwise, k7, sl m, knit to last st, p1.

Row 130 (138, 142): (WS) With D, sl 1 kwise, knit to last 8 sts, sl m, k7, p1.

Row 131 (139, 143): With L, sl 1 kwise, k7, sl m, knit to last st, p1.

Row 132 (140, 144): Sl 1 kwise, purl to last 8 sts, sl m, k7, p1.

Rep the last 4 rows until 166 (174, 182) rows have been completed, not including set-up row. Work 1 row (RS) in L, following established patt—168 (176, 184) rows total, including set-up row. Cut yarn. Place all sts on waste yarn and set aside. Carefully remove waste yarn from provisional CO and place these sts on another length of waste yarn.

BACK

Work same as front, but shape neck according to Back Neck chart (page 69) as foll: Beg with WS Row 48 (52, 56) of chart, dec 1 st at beg of next 4 WS rows—92 (96, 108) sts rem. Work even in patt until Row 112 (116, 120) has been completed. Beg with the next row (Row 113 [117, 121] of chart), inc 1 st at end of next 4 RS rows—96 (100, 112) sts. Cont in patt until a total of 168 (176, 184) rows have been worked. Cut yarn. Place sts on waste yarn. Carefully remove waste yarn from provisional CO and place these sts on another length of waste yarn.

JOIN SHOULDERS

With RS facing, pin front and back shoulder edges tog, carefully matching stripes. With D threaded on a tapestry needle and using a mattress st (see Techniques, page 140), sew front to back at shoulders.

SLEEVES

Note: Placement of block pattern and shaping of sleeve happen at the same time; read the following instructions all the way through before beginning.

Right sleeve

With RS of back facing, count 58 (58, 65) sts from the lower edge (not the neck edge), and place marker after this st to identify base of underarm. Working from this st toward shoulder seam, slip the next 38 (42, 47) sts onto a straight needle, then slip the first 38 (42, 47) front sts onto the same needle, working from shoulder seam towards lower front edge—76 (84, 94) sts total. Remove waste yarn from these sts—58 (58, 65) back sts rem on waste yarn and 58 (58, 65) front sts rem on waste yarn to be worked later. Work as foll:

Set-up row: (WS) Join L at first st on needle (above the front underarm marker), sl 1 kwise, p75 (83, 93)—2 L rows

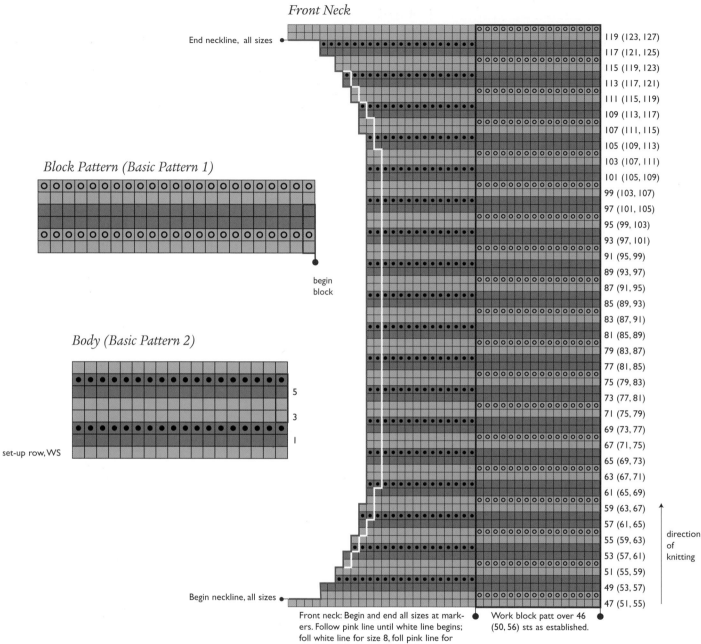

Front Neck

End neckline, all sizes

Block Pattern (Basic Pattern 1)

begin block

Body (Basic Pattern 2)

5
3
1

set-up row, WS

Begin neckline, all sizes

119 (123, 127)
117 (121, 125)
115 (119, 123)
113 (117, 121)
111 (115, 119)
109 (113, 117)
107 (111, 115)
105 (109, 113)
103 (107, 111)
101 (105, 109)
99 (103, 107)
97 (101, 105)
95 (99, 103)
93 (97, 101)
91 (95, 99)
89 (93, 97)
87 (91, 95)
85 (89, 93)
83 (87, 91)
81 (85, 89)
79 (83, 87)
77 (81, 85)
75 (79, 83)
73 (77, 81)
71 (75, 79)
69 (73, 77)
67 (71, 75)
65 (69, 73)
63 (67, 71)
61 (65, 69)
59 (63, 67)
57 (61, 65)
55 (59, 63)
53 (57, 61)
51 (55, 59)
49 (53, 57)
47 (51, 55)

direction of knitting

Front neck: Begin and end all sizes at markers. Follow pink line until white line begins; foll white line for size 8, foll pink line for sizes 4 and 6.

Work block patt over 46 (50, 56) sts as established.

Back Neck

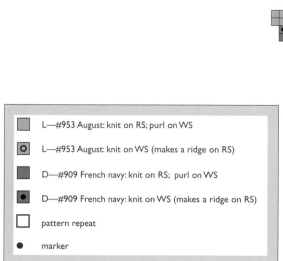

L—#953 August: knit on RS; purl on WS

L—#953 August: knit on WS (makes a ridge on RS)

D—#909 French navy: knit on RS; purl on WS

D—#909 French navy: knit on WS (makes a ridge on RS)

pattern repeat

marker

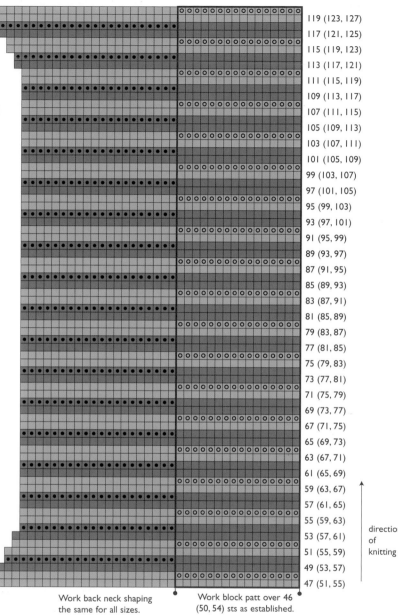

119 (123, 127)
117 (121, 125)
115 (119, 123)
113 (117, 121)
111 (115, 119)
109 (113, 117)
107 (111, 115)
105 (109, 113)
103 (107, 111)
101 (105, 109)
99 (103, 107)
97 (101, 105)
95 (99, 103)
93 (97, 101)
91 (95, 99)
89 (93, 97)
87 (91, 95)
85 (89, 93)
83 (87, 91)
81 (85, 89)
79 (83, 87)
77 (81, 85)
75 (79, 83)
73 (77, 81)
71 (75, 79)
69 (73, 77)
67 (71, 75)
65 (69, 73)
63 (67, 71)
61 (65, 69)
59 (63, 67)
57 (61, 65)
55 (59, 63)
53 (57, 61)
51 (55, 59)
49 (53, 57)
47 (51, 55)

direction
of
knitting

Work back neck shaping
the same for all sizes.

Work block patt over 46
(50, 54) sts as established.

above the underarm markers (the first L row was worked at the front and back side edge); these count as the first 2 sleeve rows.

Row 3: (RS) With D, sl 1 kwise, knit to last st, p1.

Row 4: (WS) Sl 1 kwise, knit to last st (to form a D ridge), p1.

Row 5: With L, sl 1 kwise, knit to last st, p1.

Row 6: Sl 1 kwise, purl to end of row.

Rep Rows 3–6, and *at the same time* dec 1 st each end of needle every 6 (7, 6)th row 18 (16, 21) times, then every 0 (3rd, 7th) row 0 (2, 1) time(s) as foll: sl 1, ssk (see Techniques, page 137), work in patt to last 3 sts, k2tog, p1—2 sts decreased. *Also at the same time,* after completing Row 24 (28, 36) in D (counting rows from armhole pick-up) with 68 (76, 82) sts on needle, work center 20 (24, 32) sts according to Block Pattern chart (page 68) as foll:

Row 25 (29, 37): (RS) With L, sl 1 kwise, k23 (25, 24), pm, k20 (24, 32), pm, k23 (25, 24), p1.

Row 26 (30, 38): (WS) Sl 1 kwise, p23 (25, 24), sl m, k20 (24, 32), sl m, p23 (25, 24), p1.

Row 27 (31, 39): With D, sl 1 kwise, knit to last st, p1.

Row 28 (32, 40): Sl 1 kwise, k23 (25, 24), sl m, p20 (24, 32), sl m, k23 (25, 24), p1.

Rep the last 4 rows, working decs as established, working sts outside markers in established body patt, and working center 20 (24, 32) sts in block patt until a total of 34 (46, 50) rows of block patt have been worked, ending the block patt with 2 rows L. Cont working decs as established, work all sts in established body patt. When all decs have been completed, 40 (48, 50) sts rem. Work even until sleeve has a total of 110 (118, 134) rows, ending with 2 rows L. Join D and knit all sts for 7 rows (garter st), ending with a RS row.

Next row: With WS facing, BO all sts kwise.

Left sleeve

With RS of front facing, count 58 (58, 65) sts from the lower edge (not the neck edge), and place marker after this st to identify base of underarm. Working from this st toward shoulder seam, slip the next 38 (42, 47) sts onto a straight needle, then slip the first 38 (42, 47) back sts onto the same needle, working from shoulder seam toward lower front edge—76 (84, 94) sts total. Remove waste yarn from these sts—58 (58, 65) front sts rem on waste yarn and 58 (58, 65) back sts rem on waste yarn. Beg with set-up row, work as for right sleeve.

FINISHING

Neck edging: With RS facing, D, smaller cir needle, and beg at left shoulder seam, pick up and knit 97 (97, 105) sts evenly spaced around the neck opening. Knit 10 rows. BO all sts loosely. Edging will roll forward to expose purl sts.

Seams: With RS facing, D threaded on tapestry needle, and using the mattress st (see Techniques, page 140), sew sleeve seams, carefully matching stripes.

Side seams: Working one side edge at a time, place 58 (58, 65) held front sts on one knitting needle and 58 (58, 65) held back sts on another knitting needle (remove waste yarn as you do so). With L threaded on a tapestry needle and using the Kitchener st (see Techniques, page 139), graft front to back along the side seams, using Kitchener-for-garter st to graft the 8 border sts and Kitchener-for-St st to graft the rem sts—3 rows of L at each side edge. If necessary, use the tapestry needle to tighten the grafting yarn to match the gauge of the knitting (pull the grafting yarn slightly tighter, but not so tight as to cause the work to pucker) and to make the graft less noticeable. Alternatively, with L and WS facing, join the side seams with a three-needle bind-off (see Techniques, page 135).

Weave in all loose ends to WS and secure. Block to measurements according to schematic on page 66.

FINISHED SIZE

36 (44, 50)" (91.5 [112, 127] cm) chest/bust circumference. Sweater shown measures 36" (91.5 cm).

YARN

DK-weight yarn. Sweater requires about 875 (1125, 1375) yd (800 [1028, 1257] m) dark yarn (D), and 375 (500, 625) yd (342 [457, 571] m) each of 2 light yarns (L1 and L2). We used Rowan Wool Cotton (50% wool, 50% cotton; 125 yd [113 m]/50 g): #909 French navy (D), 7 (9, 11) balls; #949 aqua (L1) and #946 elf (L2), 3 (4, 5) balls each.

NEEDLES

US Size 2 (3 mm): straight for sleeves; sizes 1 (2.5 mm) and 2 (3 mm): 16" (40-cm) and 32"(80-cm) circular (cir) for body and borders. Adjust needle size if necessary to obtain the correct gauge.

NOTIONS

US size C/2 (2.75 mm) crochet hook; markers (m); tapestry needle; six (eight, ten) ⅝" (1.5-cm) buttons; sharp-point sewing needle and matching thread; long sewing pins; 2–3 yd (1.82-2.74 m) smooth, cotton waste yarn for provisional CO and to use as stitch holders.

GAUGE

25 sts and 44 rows = 4" (10 cm) in block pattern on size 2 (3-mm) needles.

BLOCK PULLOVER

. . . .

This stylish, relaxed-fit sweater features a stripe-and-block shadow pattern, garter-stitch borders, side vents, and a square neckline. This design is easy to knit and fun to wear.

NOTES

Before beginning, review Tips—Before You Knit, pages 11-14; Abbreviations, page 134; and Techniques, pages 135-140.

The front and back of this sweater are worked flat from side to side, then the sleeve stitches are picked up along the arm edges and worked downward from the dropped shoulder to the wrist. See schematic on page 74.

The chart for this project is on page 76. The pattern repeat is 20 stitches wide and 40 rows long, and consists of four blocks, each 10 stitches wide and 20 rows long; colors D and L1 alternate on the first 20 rows, colors D and L2 alternate on the second 20 rows.

Except for the first row, one edge st is worked at each side of all rows, as follows: slip 1 knitwise at beg of row, purl 1 at end of row. On the first row, work the edge stitches the same as rest of the row. Edge stitches are not shown on charts.

Instructions are given for the smallest size

with larger sizes in parentheses. If there is only one number, it applies to all sizes.

BACK

With crochet hook, waste cotton yarn, and using the crochet method (see Techniques, page 136), provisionally CO 122 (142, 162) sts—120 (140, 160) back sts plus 1 edge st each end of needle. Join L1, and with size 2 (3-mm) needle, work Row 1 of Block chart (page 76) as foll: K122 (142, 162) sts. *Next row:* Sl 1 (edge st), work next 120 (140, 160) sts according to Row 2 of chart, p1 (edge st). Keeping 1 edge st each end of needle as established (see Notes), work through Row 40 one (one, two) time(s), then work Row 1 through Row 23 (35, 9)—63 (75, 89) rows total; piece should measure about 5¾ (7, 8)" (14.5 [18, 20.5] cm) from provisional CO.

Shape neck

Beg with Row 24 (36, 10) of chart, work as foll: BO 4 sts at the beg of row—118 (138, 158) sts rem. Re-establish 1 edge st at neck edge, cont as charted for 70 (86, 98) rows, ending with Row 14 (2, 28) of chart. *Next row:* (RS Row 15 [3, 29] of chart) Work to

end of row, then use backward loop method (see Techniques, page 135) to CO 4 sts to complete neck—122 (142, 162) sts; 135 (163, 189) rows total from provisional CO; neck opening should measure about 6½ (8, 9)" (16.5 [20.5, 23] cm) wide; piece will measure about 12¼ (15, 17)" (31 [38, 43] cm) from provisional CO.

Re-establish 1 edge st at neck edge and cont as charted until a total of 198 (238, 278) rows have been worked from provisional CO, ending last rep with 2 rows of L2 (the final 2 rows of D will be worked later as part of the sleeve and side edge sts). The back will be complete after Rows 1–40 of chart have been worked a total of 4 (5, 6) times, and Rows 1–38 have been worked once more—198 (238, 278) rows total; piece should measure about 18 (22, 25)" (45.5 [56, 63.5] cm) from beg. Place all sts on waste yarn, tie ends of waste yarn tog to secure, and set aside. Carefully remove waste yarn from provisional CO and secure these 122 (142, 162) sts on another length of waste yarn.

FRONT

Work as back to beg of neck shaping—piece should measure about 5¾ (7, 8)" (14.5 [18, 20.5] cm) from provisional CO.

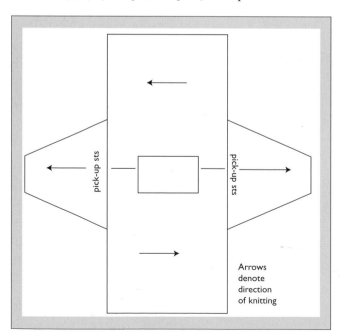

pick-up sts

pick-up sts

Arrows denote direction of knitting

Shape neck

Beg with Row 24 (36, 10) of chart, BO 21 (22, 22) sts at beg of row (neck edge)—101 (120, 140) sts rem. Re-establish 1 edge st at neck edge, cont as charted until Rows 1–40 have been worked a total of 3 (4, 4) times, then work Rows 1–15 (3, 29) once—piece should measure about 12¼ (15, 17)" (31 [38, 43] cm) from provisional CO. At the end of the last row worked (RS Row 15 [3, 29]), use the backward loop method to CO 21 (22, 22) sts—122 (142, 162) sts; 135 (163, 189) rows total from provisional CO.

Re-establish 1 edge st at neck edge and cont as charted until piece measures same as back—198 (238, 278) rows total, ending last rep with 2 rows of L2 (the final 2 rows of D are worked later as part of the sleeve and side edge sts). Place all sts on waste yarn as for back. Carefully remove waste yarn from provisional CO and secure these sts on another length of waste yarn.

SHOULDER SEAMS

Hold front and back with RS facing. Pin tog at shoulder edges, matching D stripes and lining up L1 stripes on one piece with L2 stripes on the other. With D threaded on tapestry needle and using the mattress stitch (see Techniques, page 140), sew shoulders tog, working just inside the edge sts and being careful not to catch the live sts on waste-yarn holders. Remove pins.

SLEEVES

Right sleeve

(Worked in D and L2) With RS of front facing, count up 72 (85, 101) sts from the lower edge (not the neck edge), place marker after this st to identify base of underarm. Working from this st toward shoulder seam, slip the next 50 (57, 61) sts onto a straight needle, then slip the first 50 (57, 61) back sts onto the same needle, working from shoulder seam towards lower back edge—100 (114, 122) sts total. Place marker after last st to identify base of underarm. Remove waste yarn from these sts—72 (85, 101) front sts rem on waste yarn and 72 (85, 101) back sts rem on waste yarn to be worked later. Beg with 2 rows of D, work sleeve in Basic Pattern 2 (page 7) as foll:

Row 1: (RS) Join D, sl 1 kwise, k98 (112, 120), p1.

Row 2: (WS) Sl 1 kwise, knit to last st, p1 (D ridge formed on RS).

Row 3: Join L2, sl 1 kwise, knit to last st, p1.

Row 4: Sl 1 kwise, purl to end of row.

Rep Rows 1–4 throughout sleeve for a total of 160 (168, 180) rows, ending with 2 rows L2. *At the same time,* dec 1 st each end of needle (sl 1, ssk, work in patt to last 3 sts, k2tog, p1) every 6th row 20 (28, 28) times, then every 8 (0, 10)th row 5 (0, 1) time(s)—50 (58, 64) sts rem. Cut off L2. With D, knit 7 rows, ending with a RS row. With WS facing, BO all sts kwise. Leave armhole markers in place.

Left sleeve

(worked with D and L1) With RS of back facing, count up 72 (85, 101) sts from lower edge (not the neck edge), place marker after this st to identify base of underarm. Working from this st toward shoulder seam, slip the next 50 (57, 61) sts onto a straight needle, then slip the first 50 (57, 61) front sts onto the same needle, working from shoulder toward the lower front edge—100 (114, 122) sts total. Place marker after last st to identify base of underarm. Remove waste yarn from these sts—72 (85, 101) front sts rem on waste yarn and 72 (85, 101) back sts rem on waste yarn. Work as for right sleeve, substituting L1 for L2. Leave armhole markers in place.

FINISHING

Lower body edging: With RS facing, size 1 (2.5 mm) 32" (80-cm) cir needle, and working from the lower right front edge toward underarm marker, slip 72 (85, 101) sts from front waste yarn onto needle. Join D at underarm

Block

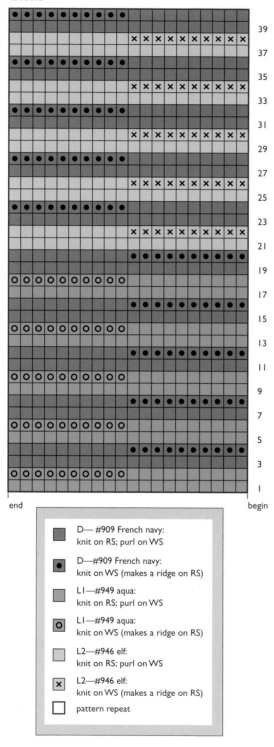

end   begin

■	D— #909 French navy: knit on RS; purl on WS
⊙	D—#909 French navy: knit on WS (makes a ridge on RS)
▨	L1—#949 aqua: knit on RS; purl on WS
⊚	L1—#949 aqua: knit on WS (makes a ridge on RS)
▨	L2—#946 elf: knit on RS; purl on WS
☒	L2—#946 elf: knit on WS (makes a ridge on RS)
☐	pattern repeat

marker, knit these 72 (85, 101) sts, working from the underarm marker to the lower edge, place marker (pm), pick up and knit 1 st at the corner, pm, then working across lower front edge, pick up and knit 99 (119, 139) sts (about 1 st for every 2 rows), pm, pick up and knit 1 st in corner, pm, temporarily place 72 (85, 101) sts from waste yarn on another needle, then knit these sts—245 (291, 343) sts total; 4 markers placed. Working back and forth in rows, knit 7 rows, and *at the same time* inc 1 st each side of each marker every RS row as foll: Knit to 1 st before marker, *k1f&b, slip marker (sl m), k1 (corner st), sl m, k1f&b; rep from * at each corner—8 sts increased each RS row; 24 stitches increased total. Work all WS rows even without increasing. With WS facing, BO all sts kwise. Remove markers.

Neck edging: With D, 16″ (40-cm) cir needle, RS facing, and beg at left shoulder seam, pick up and knit 21 (23, 23) sts along left side of neck, pm, pick up and knit 1 st in corner, pm, pick up and knit 36 (44, 50) sts (about 1 st for every 2 rows) across front neck edge, pm, pick up and knit 1 st in corner, pm, pick up and knit 21 (23, 23) sts along right side of front neck, pick up and knit 3 sts along back right side neck, pm, pick up and knit 1 st in corner, pm, pick up and knit 36 (44, 50) sts across back neck, pm, pick up and knit 1 st in corner, pm, pick up and knit 3 sts along left side edge of back neck—124 (144, 156) sts total; 8 markers placed. Join for working in the rnd. *Purl 1 rnd, knit 1 rnd; rep from * 4 times, and *at the same time* dec 1 st each side of each marker every knit rnd as foll: Knit to 2 sts before marker, *ssk (see Techniques, page 137), sl m, k1 (corner st) sl m, k2tog; rep from * at each corner—8 sts decreased per rnd; 32 sts decreased after 4 knit rnds; 92 (112, 124) sts rem. BO all sts loosely pwise.

Side seams: With RS of front facing and working on the left side just below underarm marker, lap the front garter-st side border over back garter-st side border. Pin side borders tog, leaving the last 2 blocks (20 sts) at lower edge open.

With just 2 plies of D threaded on a tapestry needle, and working from underarm marker toward lower edge, use a backstich to sew (see Techniques, page 138) to sew the side borders tog, leaving the last two blocks open and working the seam "in the ditch" between the last two purl ridges.

Buttons: The buttons are simply an optional decorative feature; no buttonholes are required. With sewing needle and thread, attach one button to the garter-st side border one block (10 sts) down from underarm marker, sewing through both layers of side borders. *Sew the next button to the side border at the end of the next 2 squares; rep from * until 3 (4, 5) buttons have been used. Rep for the other side.

Sleeve seams: With D threaded on a tapestry needle and using the mattress st, sew sleeve seams.

Turn work to WS and weave in loose ends through several sts and secure. Remove rem markers and all waste yarns. Block sweater to measurements (see below) and lightly steam seams and borders.

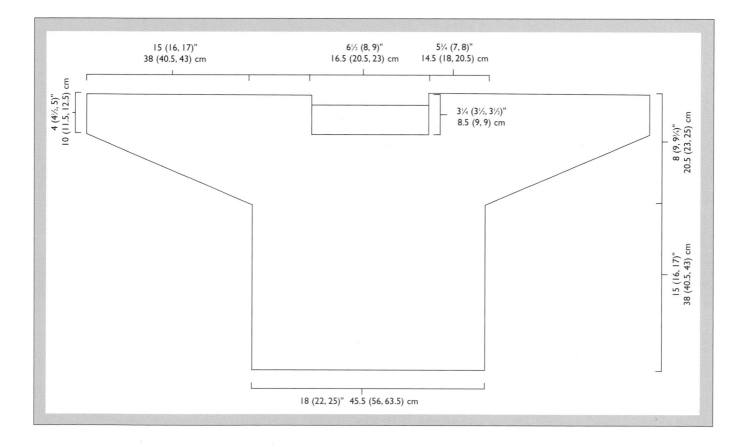

WOMAN'S VERSION

FINISHED SIZE

40½ (44, 47, 50, 54, 57)" (103 [112, 119.5, 127, 137, 145] cm) bust/chest circumference. Sweater shown measures 47" (119.5 cm).

YARN

Fingering-weight yarn. Sweater requires about 1085 (1085, 1302, 1302, 1302, 1302) yd (995 [995, 1194, 1194, 1194, 1194] m) dark yarn (D), 651 yd (595 m) light yarn (L1), and 1085 (1085, 1085, 1085, 1302, 1302) yd (995 [995, 995, 995, 1194, 1194] m) of another light yarn (L2).

We suggest Harrisville Designs New England Shetland (100% pure virgin wool; 217 yd [198 m]/50 g): #85 ebony (D), 5 (5, 6, 6, 6, 6) skeins; #49 charcoal (L1), 3 skeins (all sizes); #45 pearl (L2), 5 (5, 5, 5, 6, 6) skeins.

NEEDLES

Sizes 1 and 2 (2.5 mm and 3 mm): straight. Size 1 (2.5 mm): 24" (60-cm) circular (cir) for neck edging. Adjust needle size if necessary to obtain the correct gauge.

NOTIONS

Markers (m); tapestry needle.

GAUGE

24 sts and 46 rows = 4" (10 cm) in stripes pattern with size 2 (3 mm) needles.

see page 84 for Man's Version

TONE-ON-TONE SWEATERS

for her and him

. . . .

Perfect for men or women, Tone-on-Tone is a simple, classic, and lovely everyday sweater. It is knit from the bottom up, with the back, front, and sleeves each worked separately. You may choose a cowl collar for her or a V-neck style for him.

NOTES

Before beginning, review Tips—Before You Knit, pages 11–14; Abbreviations, page 134; Techniques, pages 135–140.

The charts for this project are on page 83. There is one edge stitch at each end of needle that is not shown on charts. Work the edge stitches as follows: Slip 1 knitwise at the beginning of every row, purl 1 at the end of every row, except for the first row. Work all sts in the first row after CO as directed.

This project requires simultaneous color and chart changes and shaping; read the instructions all the way through to the end before beginning a section.

Instructions are given for the smallest size with the larger sizes in parentheses.

If there is only one number, it applies to all sizes.

The yarn for this design can be purchased as a kit. See Resources, page 142 for more information.

FOR HER

BACK

With L1 and larger straight needles, CO 122 (132, 142, 152, 162, 172) sts.

Lower edging
Row 1: (RS) K122 (132, 142, 152, 162, 172).
Row 2: Sl 1 (edge st), k120 (130, 140, 150, 160, 170), p1 (edge st).
Working edge sts as established (see Notes), knit rem sts for 11 more rows (7 ridges on RS), ending with a WS row.
Next row: (RS) Working edge sts as

Woman's Version

established, join D and work Rows 1–4 of Edging chart (page 83) across center 120 (130, 140, 150, 160, 170) sts 12 times—48 rows total; 12 ridges of L1 on RS. With D, work Rows 1 and 2 again—50 rows of chart worked.

Body
Maintaining edge sts as established, change to L2 and D and beg as indicated for women's sizes, work center 120 (130, 140, 150, 160, 170) sts according to Stripes chart (page 83) until piece measures 22½ (24, 25½, 27, 28¾, 30)" (57 [61, 65, 68.5, 73, 76] cm) from CO, ending with 2 rows of L2.

Shoulder edging
Maintaining edge sts as established, change to L1 and D.

Work Rows 1–4 of Edging chart until piece measures 23½ (25, 26½, 28, 29¾, 31)" (59.5 [63.5, 67.5, 71, 75.5, 78.5] cm) from CO, ending with a WS row.

Shape neck
(RS) Work 46 (51, 55, 60, 64, 69) sts in patt, join new yarn and BO the center 30 (30, 32, 32, 34, 34) sts, work to end of row—46 (51, 55, 60, 64, 69) sts rem at each side. Working each side separately and cont working Edging chart, shape neck as foll: At each neck edge, BO 4 sts once—42 (47, 51, 56, 60, 65) sts rem each side. At each neck edge, BO 1 st once—41 (46, 50, 55, 59, 64) sts rem.

Shape shoulders
Cont working each side separately as established, at each armhole edge BO 13 (15, 16, 18, 19, 21) sts once, then BO

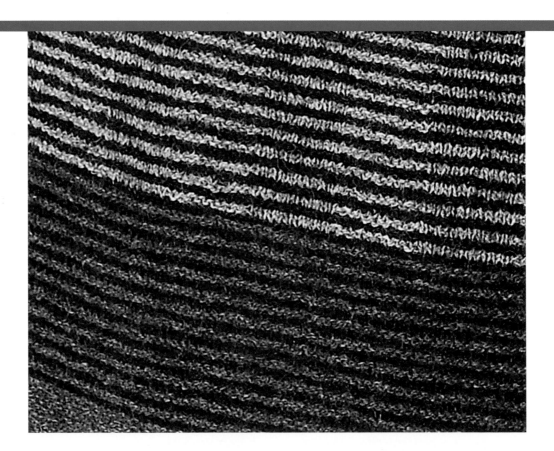

14 (15, 17, 18, 20, 21) sts once, then BO rem 14 (16, 17, 19, 20, 22) sts.

FRONT

Work as for back until piece measures 22 (23½, 24½, 26, 27¼, 28½)″ (56 [59.5, 62, 66, 69, 72.5] cm) from CO edge, ending with a WS row.

Shape neck

Note: The neck and shoulders are shaped at the same time as the pattern shifts from Stripes chart to Edging chart; read the following instructions all the way through to the end before beginning. (RS) Work 56 (61, 65, 70, 74, 79) sts in patt, join new yarn and BO the center 10 (10, 12, 12, 14,

14) sts, work to end of row—56 (61, 65, 70, 74, 79) sts rem each side. Working each side separately, cont in patt as established, and *at the same time,* at each neck edge, BO 3 sts once, then BO 2 sts 2 times, then BO 1 st 8 times—41 (46, 50, 55, 59, 64) sts rem each side; 23 rows total from neck BO. *Also at the same time,* when piece measures 22½ (24, 25½, 27, 28¾, 30)″ (57 [61, 65, 68.5, 73, 76] cm) from CO, ending with 2 rows in L2, change to L1 and D, and beg with Row 1, work Edging chart as for back shoulder until piece measures same length as back to beg of shoulder shaping (count the number of ridges on each piece).

Shape shoulders

Cont working each side separately as established, at each

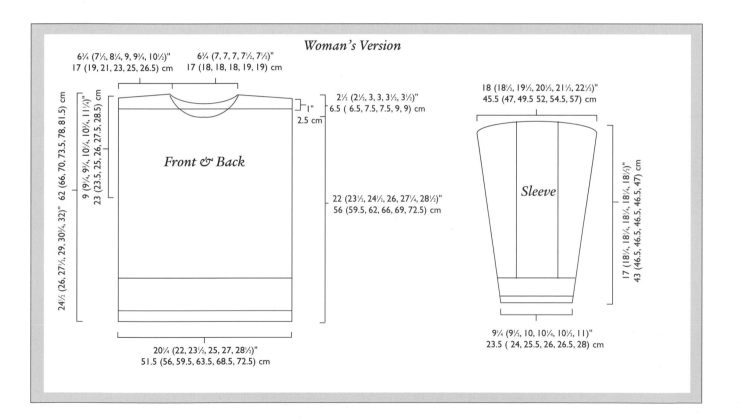

Woman's Version

6¾ (7½, 8¼, 9, 9¾, 10½)″
17 (19, 21, 23, 25, 26.5) cm

6¾ (7, 7, 7, 7½, 7½)″
17 (18, 18, 18, 19, 19) cm

2½ (2½, 3, 3, 3½, 3½)″
6.5 (6.5, 7.5, 7.5, 9, 9) cm

1″
2.5 cm

9 (9¾, 9¾, 10¼, 10¾, 11¼)″
23 (23.5, 25, 26, 27.5, 28.5) cm

24½ (26, 27½, 29, 30¼, 32)″ 62 (66, 70, 73.5, 78, 81.5) cm

Front & Back

22 (23½, 24½, 26, 27¼, 28½)″
56 (59.5, 62, 66, 69, 72.5) cm

20¼ (22, 23½, 25, 27, 28½)″
51.5 (56, 59.5, 63.5, 68.5, 72.5) cm

18 (18½, 19½, 20½, 21½, 22½)″
45.5 (47, 49.5 52, 54.5, 57) cm

Sleeve

17 (18¼, 18¼, 18¼, 18¼, 18½)″
43 (46.5, 46.5, 46.5, 46.5, 47) cm

9¼ (9½, 10, 10¼, 10½, 11)″
23.5 (24, 25.5, 26, 26.5, 28) cm

armhole edge, BO 13 (15, 16, 18, 19, 21) sts once, then BO 14 (15, 17, 18, 20, 21) sts once, then BO rem 14 (16, 17, 19, 20, 22) sts.

SLEEVES

Lower edging

With L1 and smaller needles, CO 56 (58, 60, 62, 64, 66) sts. *Next row:* (RS) K56 (58, 60, 62, 64, 66). *Next row:* Sl 1 kwise (edge st), k54 (56, 58, 60, 62, 64), p1 (edge st). Working edge sts as established (see Notes), knit rem sts for 11 more rows (7 ridges on RS), ending with a WS row. Change to larger needles and cont working edge sts as established, join D and work Rows 1–4 of Edging chart until there are 9 ridges of L1 on RS, ending with 2 rows of D—38 rows of chart worked.

Sleeve body

Place 3 markers (pm) as foll: one after 28 (29, 30, 31, 32, 33) sts to mark the center of row, one 10 sts before the center marker, and one 10 sts after the center marker—2 outside markers with 20 sts between them, plus 1 marker in the center of these 20 sts. Change to L2 and D and, keeping edge sts as established, work rem sts according to Rows 1–4 of Sleeve chart (*Note:* Edge sts and increases are not shown on chart). *At the same time,* counting from the first D row in Sleeve chart, shape sleeve as foll: inc 1 st each end of needle (inside edge sts) on the 9 (15, 13, 11, 9, 7, 7)th row once, then every 8 (10, 8, 8, 6, 6)th row 10 (1, 7, 2, 30, 27) time(s), then every 6 (8, 6, 6, 4, 4)th row 15 (10, 21, 28, 2, 7) times, then every 0 (6, 0, 0, 0, 0)th row 0 (15, 0, 0, 0, 0) times, working new sts into established patt of dark ridges on a light background before the marked 20 center sts and as light ridges on a dark background after the marked center sts—108 (112, 118, 124, 130, 136) sts. Cont in patt until piece measures about 16½ (17¾, 17¾, 17¾, 17¾, 18)" (42 [45, 45, 45, 45, 45.5] cm) from CO, or 5 rows less than desired total sleeve length.

Shape cap

BO 16 (16, 17, 17, 18, 18) sts at the beg of next 4 rows—44 (48, 50, 56, 58, 64) sts rem. BO all sts.

FINISHING

Join shoulders: With yarn threaded on a tapestry needle and using the invisible horizontal seam (see Techniques, page 139), sew shoulders tog.

Cowl collar: With RS facing, cir needle, and D, pick up and knit 46 (46, 48, 48, 50, 50) sts across back neck and 64 (64, 70, 70, 76, 76) sts around front neck—110 (110, 118, 118, 126, 126) sts total. Do not join. Purl 1 row. Change to L1, join sts into a rnd, and work 4 rnds as foll: *K1, sl 1 kwise with yarn in front; rep from *. Change to D and knit 1 rnd, inc 23 sts evenly spaced—133 (133, 141, 141, 149, 149) sts. Turn work, and with WS facing, cont as foll: *With D, knit 2 rnds. With L1, knit 1 rnd, then purl 1 rnd; rep from * until there are 17 L1 ridges on RS of cowl. With D, knit 2 rnds. With L1, [knit 1 rnd, purl 1 rnd] 9 times. BO all sts pwise.

Seams: Mark center of sleeve top with a pin. Mark armhole spacing by placing a pin about 9 (9¼, 9¾, 10¼, 10¾, 11¼)" (23 [23.5, 25, 26, 27.5, 28.5] cm) down from the shoulder seam, along the side edge of the front and back. With RS tog, match center of sleeve top to shoulder seam, and top edge of sleeve between armhole markers. Pin sleeves in place and use yarn threaded on a tapestry needle to sew sleeves in place. With RS facing and using the mattress st, sew sleeve and sides seams, carefully aligning patt ridges. Remove pins. Weave all loose ends to WS of work and secure.

Edging

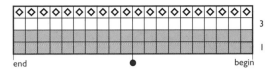

end   begin

3

1

Stripes

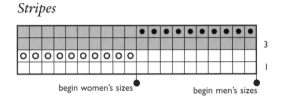

3

1

begin women's sizes   begin men's sizes

Sleeve

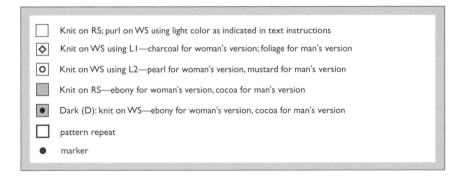

3

1

Work sts after marked center sts as light ridges on a dark background.

Work center 20 sts in Stripes pattern.

Work sts before marked center sts as dark ridges on a light background.

☐	Knit on RS; purl on WS using light color as indicated in text instructions
◇	Knit on WS using L1—charcoal for woman's version; foliage for man's version
○	Knit on WS using L2—pearl for woman's version, mustard for man's version
▨	Knit on RS—ebony for woman's version, cocoa for man's version
⊡	Dark (D): knit on WS—ebony for woman's version, cocoa for man's version
☐	pattern repeat
●	marker

MAN'S VERSION
FINISHED SIZE
44 (47, 50, 54, 57)" (112 [119.5, 127, 137, 145] cm) chest circumference. Sweater shown measures 47" (119.5 cm).

YARN
Fingering-weight yarn. Sweater requires about 1085 (1302, 1302, 1302, 1302) yd (995 [1194, 1194, 1194, 1194] m) dark yarn (D), 651 yd (595 m) light yarn (L1), and 1085 (1085, 1085, 1302, 1302) yd (995, [995, 995, 1194, 1194] m) of another light yarn (L2).
We suggest Harrisville Designs New England Shetland (100% pure virgin wool; 217 yd [198 m]/50 g): #37 cocoa (D), 5 (6, 6, 6, 6) skeins; #80 foliage (L1), 3 skeins (all sizes); #81 mustard (L2), 5 (5, 5, 6, 6) skeins.

NEEDLES
Sizes 1 and 2 (2.5 mm and 3 mm): straight. Size 1 (2.5 mm): 24" (60-cm) circular (cir) for neck edging. Size 4 (3.5 mm): two double-pointed (dpn) for I-cord. Adjust needle size if necessary to obtain the correct gauge.

NOTIONS
Markers (m); tapestry needle.

GAUGE
24 sts and 46 rows = 4" (10 cm) in stripes pattern with size 2 (3 mm) needles.

FOR HIM
NOTES
Before beginning, review Tips—Before You Knit, pages 11–14; Abbreviations, page 134; Techniques, pages 135–140.

The charts for this project are on page 83. There is one edge stitch at each end of needle that is not shown on charts. Work the edge stitches as follows: Slip 1 knitwise at the beginning of every row, purl 1 at the end of every row.

This project requires simultaneous color and chart changes and shaping; read the instructions all the way through to the end before beginning a section.

Instructions are given for the smallest size with larger sizes in parentheses. If there is only one number, it applies to all sizes.

The yarn for this design maybe purchased as a kit. See Resources, page 142 for more information.

BACK
With L1 and larger straight needles, CO 132 (142, 152, 162, 172) sts.

Lower edging
Change to smaller needles and work the first row in k1, p1 rib, then work rib with edge sts as foll: Sl 1 (edge st), *k1, p1; rep from * to last st, p1 (edge st). Working edge sts as established (see Notes), cont in established rib until piece measures 1½" (3.8 cm) from beg, ending with a WS row.

Working edge sts as established, join D and work Rows 1–4 of Edging chart (page 83) across center 130 (140, 150, 160, 170) sts 12 times—48 rows total; 12 ridges of L1 on RS. With D, work Rows 1 and 2 again—50 rows of chart worked.

Body
Maintaining edge sts as established, change to L2 and D, and beg as indicated for men's sizes, work center 130 (140, 150, 160, 170) sts according to Stripes chart (page 83) until piece measures 24 (25½, 27, 28¾, 30)" (61 [65, 68.5, 73, 76] cm) from CO edge, ending with 2 rows of L2.

Shoulder edging
Maintaining edge sts as established, change to L1 and D. Work Rows 1–4 of Edging chart until piece measures 25 (26½, 28, 29¾, 31)" (63.5 [67.5, 71, 75.5, 78.5] cm) from CO edge, ending with a WS row.

Shape neck
(RS) Work 51 (55, 60, 64, 69) sts in patt, join new yarn and BO the center 30 (32, 32, 34, 34) sts, work to end of row—51 (55, 60, 64, 69) sts rem at each side. Working each side separately and cont working Edging chart, shape neck as foll: At each neck edge, BO 4 sts once—47 (51, 56, 60, 65) sts rem each side. At each neck edge, BO 1 st once—46 (50, 55, 59, 64) sts rem each side. Work 2 rows even.

Shape shoulders
Cont working each side separately as established, at each armhole edge, BO 15

Man's Version

(16, 18, 19, 21) sts once, then BO 15 (17, 18, 20, 21) sts once, then BO rem 16 (17, 19, 20, 22) sts.

FRONT

Work as for back until piece measures 15¾ (17, 18½, 20, 21¼)" (40 [43, 47, 51, 54] cm) from CO edge, ending with a WS row.

Shape V-neck

Note: The neck and shoulders are shaped at the same time as the pattern shifts from Stripes chart to Edging chart; read the following instructions all the way through to the end before beginning. (RS) Work 65 (70, 75, 80, 85) sts in patt, place the 2 center sts on a small stitch holder or short strand of waste yarn for base of V, join new yarn and work to end—65 (70, 75, 80, 85) sts at each side. Working each side separately, cont in patt as established for 3 rows, ending with a WS row. Then cont as foll:

Right side neck and shoulder (as worn on body)

(RS) Sl 1 kwise (edge st), ssk (see Techniques, page 137), work in patt to end of needle—1 st decreased. Dec 1 st at neck edge (beg of RS rows) in this manner every 4th row 1 (2, 4, 7, 7) more time(s), then every 6th row 17 (17, 15, 13, 13) times—46 (50, 55, 59, 64) sts rem. *Also at the same time,* when piece measures 24 (25½, 27, 28¾, 30)" (61 [65, 68.5, 73, 76] cm) from CO edge, ending with 2 rows of L2, change to L1 and D, and beg with Row 1, work Edging chart as for back until piece measures same length as back to beg of shoulder shaping (count the number of ridges on each piece). At armhole edge (beg of WS rows), BO 15 (16, 18, 19, 21) sts once, then BO 15 (17, 18, 20, 21) sts once, then BO rem 16 (17, 19, 20, 22) sts.

Left side neck and shoulder (as worn on body)

(RS) Sl 1 (edge st), work in patt to last 3 sts, k2tog, p1 (edge st)—1 st decreased. Dec 1 st at neck edge (end of RS rows) in this manner every 4th row 1 (2, 4, 7, 7) more time(s), then every 6th row 17 (17, 15, 13, 13) times—46 (50, 55, 59, 64) sts rem. *Also at the same time,* when piece

measures 24 (25½, 27, 28¾, 30)" (61 [65, 68.5, 73, 76] cm) from beg, ending with 2 rows of L2, change to L1 and D, and beg with Row 1, work Edging chart as for back until piece measures same length as back to beg of shoulder shaping. At armhole edge (beg of RS rows), BO 15 (16, 18, 19, 21) sts once, then BO 15 (17, 18, 20, 21) sts once, then BO rem 16 (17, 19, 20, 22) sts.

SLEEVES

Hem

With L1 and smaller needles, CO 58 (60, 62, 64, 66) sts. *Next row:* (RS) K58 (60, 62, 64, 66). *Next row:* Sl 1 (edge st), k56 (58, 60, 62, 64), p1 (edge st). Working edge sts as established (see Notes), work rem sts in St st until piece measures 1¼" (3.2 cm) from beg for facing, ending with a WS row. Purl 1 (RS) row for turning ridge. Change to larger needle and work St st for 1¼" (3.2 cm), ending with a WS row. Cont working edge sts as established, join D and work Rows 1–4 of Edging chart until there are 9 ridges of L1 on RS, ending with 2 rows of D—38 rows of chart worked.

Sleeve body

Place 3 markers (pm) as foll: one after 29 (30, 31, 32, 33) sts to mark center of row, one 10 sts before the center marker, and one 10 sts after the center marker—2 outside markers with 20 sts between them, plus 1 marker in the center of these 20 sts. Change to L2 and D, and keeping edge sts as established, work rem sts according to Rows 1–4 of Sleeve chart (*Note:* Edge sts and increases are not shown on chart). *At the same time,* counting from the first D row in Sleeve chart, shape sleeve as foll: inc 1 st each end of needle (inside edge sts) every 8th row 6 (6, 8, 8, 8) times, then every 6th row 21 (23, 23, 25, 27) times, working new sts into established patt of dark ridges on a light background before marked center sts and as light ridges on a dark background after marked center sts—112 (118, 124, 130, 136) sts. Cont in patt until piece measures 18 (18½, 19, 19¾, 20¾)" (45.5 [47, 48.5, 50, 52.5] cm) from turning ridge, or 5 rows less than desired total sleeve length.

Shape cap
BO 16 (17, 17, 18, 18) sts at beg of next 4 rows—48 (50, 56, 58, 64) sts rem. BO all sts.

FINISHING

Sleeve cuffs: Fold cuff lining to WS along turning ridge to form hem. With L1 threaded on a tapestry needle and using a whipstitch (see Techniques, page 140), sew CO edge to WS of sleeve.

Join shoulders: With yarn threaded on a tapestry needle and using the invisible horizontal seam (see Techniques, page 139), sew shoulders tog.

Neck edging: With D, cir needle, RS facing, and beg at right shoulder seam, pick up and knit 45 (47, 47, 49, 49) sts across back neck and 57 (59, 59, 61, 61) sts along left side (as worn on body) of neck, pm, k2 held sts at base of V, pm, pick up and knit 57 (59, 59, 61, 61) sts along right side of neck—161 (167, 167, 173, 173) sts total. Join for working in a rnd. Purl 1 rnd. *Next rnd:* Join L1 and *knit to 2 sts before

center front marker, k2tog, slip marker (sl m), p2, sl m, ssk (see Techniques, page 137), knit to end of rnd—2 sts decreased. Purl 1 rnd. Rep from * 5 more times (12 rnds total)—149 (155, 155, 161, 161) sts rem. Do not cut off yarn. *I-Cord edging:* With dpn and beg with the first st on the needle, use the knitted method (see Techniques, page 136) to CO 5 new sts for I-cord. With RS facing, *k4, p2tog (1 I-cord st and 1 st from cir needle), bring yarn to back of work, place next st from cir needle onto dpn, and slide sts to other end of dpn. Rep from *, always working with RS facing, until 5 sts rem. Break yarn, thread tail on a tapestry needle and use Kitchener st (see Techniques, page 139) to join rem live sts to the 5 CO sts.

Seams: Measure about 9¼ (9¾, 10¼, 10¾, 11¼)" (23.5 [25, 26, 27.5, 28.5] cm) down from shoulder seam, along side edge of front and back, and mark for sleeve placement. Match center of sleeve top to shoulder seam, and use yarn threaded on a tapestry needle to sew top edge of sleeve between markers. With RS facing, sew sleeve and side seams, aligning patt ridges. Weave in all loose ends to WS.

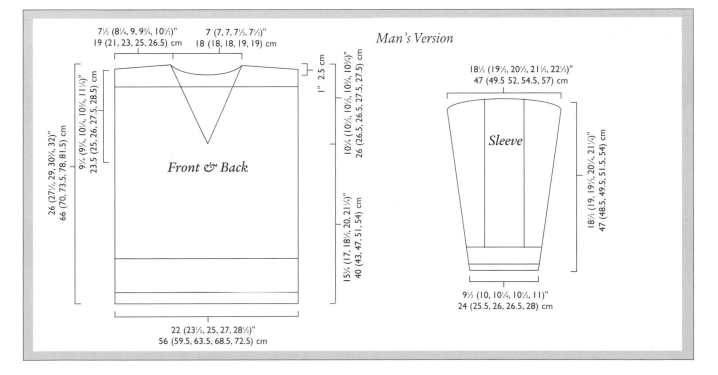

FINISHED SIZE

About 50 (57)" (127 [145] cm) bust/chest circumference, with fronts overlapped. Sweater shown measures 50" (127 cm).

YARN

Fingering-weight yarn. Jacket requires about 1300 (1500) yd (1199 [1372] m) dark yarn (D) and 217 yd [199 m] each of 9 light colors (L1–L9). We suggest Harrisville Designs New England Shetland (100% pure virgin wool; 217 yd [198 m]/50 g): #85 ebony (D), 6 (7) skeins; #84 lime (L1), #06 cornsilk (L2), #04 gold (L3), #66 melon (L4), #65 poppy (L5), #02 red (L6), #35 chianti (L7), #23 magenta (L8), and #21 violet (L9), 1 skein each.

NEEDLES

US size 1 and 2 (2.5 mm and 3 mm): straight and 32" (80-cm) circular (cir), plus an extra size 2 (3 mm) cir. Adjust needle size if necessary to obtain the correct gauge.

NOTIONS

Markers (m); about 3 yd (3 m) of waste cotton yarn to use as marking thread and stitch holder; tapestry needle.

GAUGE

24 sts and 46 rows = 4" (10 cm) in charted pattern.

This fun-to-knit jacket, in all the colors of the rainbow, is perfect for knitters who love a lot of color in their projects. The jacket is knitted in two pieces from the cuff to the center, and then grafted together at the center back with Kitchener stitch.

NOTES

Before you begin, review Tips—Before You Knit, pages 11–14; Abbreviations, page 134; Techniques, pages 135–140.

Jacket is worked sideways in two sections, each beginning with a sleeve cuff and ending at the center front and back. See schematic on page 93. Circular needles are used to accommodate the large number of stitches in the body.

The chart for this project is on page 90. The dark color (D) is used throughout; the light color (L) changes after every 20 rows to form broad stripes in Basic Pattern 1 (light ridges against a dark background) and Basic Pattern 2 (dark ridges against a light background), as described on page 7. Work the light colors in the following sequence: L1, L2, L3, L4, L5, L6, L7, L8, L9, then work the colors in reverse order: L8, L7, L6, L5, L4, L3, L2, L1.

One edge stitch is worked at each side of all rows as follows: slip 1 knitwise at beg of row, purl 1 at end of row. Edge stitches are not shown on charts.

10-stitch garter-stitch borders are worked for the lower back, lower front, and neck. Work these border stitches in the same color as used for the rest of the row. The edge stitches (sl 1 kwise at beg of row; p1 at end of row) are included in these 10 stitches. For example, if the border is worked at the beginning of a row, work as follows: Sl 1 (edge st), k9 (border sts); if the border is worked at the end of a row, work as follows: K9 (border sts), p1 (edge st).

Instructions are given for the small/medium size. The larger size is in parentheses. If there is only one number, it applies to both sizes.

The yarns for this design can be purchased as a kit. See Resources, page 142.

LEFT HALF OF JACKET

Left sleeve cuff

With D, smaller needles, and using the

long-tail method (see Techniques, page 136), CO 46 (52) sts.

Set-up row: (WS) With D, knit all sts (forms dark ridge on RS). Join L1 and work garter st as foll:

Rows 1 and 2: With L, sl 1 kwise, knit to last st, p1.

Rows 3 and 4: With D, sl 1 kwise, knit to last st, p1.

Rep Rows 1–4 until cuff measures 3″ (7.5 cm) from beg, ending with a WS row of D (dark ridge on RS). Break or cut yarns, leaving about 4″ (10-cm) tails to weave in later. Turn work so that WS of cuff will become RS of sleeve. *Note:* All further measurements and numbers of rows are counted from this point. In order to mark the center, and later the shoulder line, insert a marking thread of smooth cotton waste yarn between the 2 center sts. As you work each row, weave this thread up the center of the work to mark the shoulder line and the boundary between front and back. This thread marker follows the project through-out, and will not be mentioned in the text again until the end of sleeve.

Left sleeve

Change to larger needles, join L2 (L1), and work broad stripes of dark ridges on a light background (Basic Pattern 2) as foll:

Row 1: (RS) With L2 (L1), sl 1 kwise, knit to last st, p1.

Row 2: (WS) With L2 (L1), sl 1 kwise, purl to end of row.

Row 3: (RS) Join D, sl 1 kwise, knit to last st, p1.

Row 4: (WS) With D, sl 1 kwise, knit to end of row (forms a dark ridge on RS).

Work these 4 rows 5 times (20 rows total; 5 dark ridges on RS). *Note:* Shaping, color changes, and chart changes occur simultaneously; read the following instructions all the way through to the end before beginning. Change to L3 (L2) and D, and rep these 20 rows for second broad stripe, and *at the same time,* on the first row of the second broad stripe, inc 1 st each end of needle as foll: Sl 1 (edge st), M1 (see Techniques, page 138) work in patt to last st, M1, p1 (edge st)—2 sts increased; 48 (54) sts. Maintaining edge sts and working broad stripes as established (chang-

Rainbow Jacket

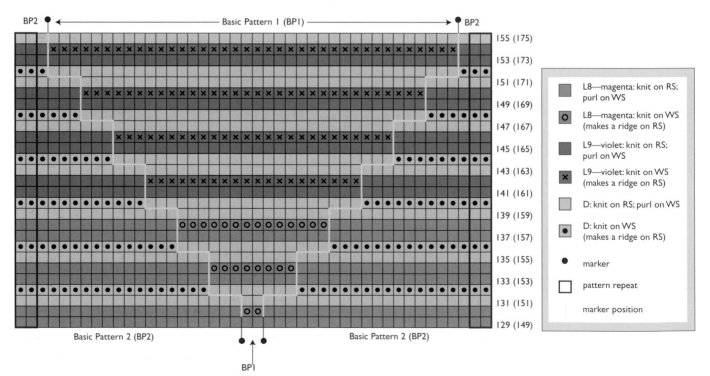

ing the light color every 20 rows as specified in Notes), inc 1 st each end of needle in this manner every 4th row 24 (29) more times—96 (112) sts; 117 (137) rows of patt worked. Then inc 1 st at the beg of every row for the rest of the sleeve. *Also at the same time,* work broad stripes color changes as described in Notes until ready to begin L8.

Begin Basic Pattern 1

Work the first 8 rows in established patt, ending after Rows 128 (148) of broad stripe L8 and D. Place marker (pm) on each side of the center 2 sts (see Rainbow Jacket chart). Cont to work Basic Pattern 2 (dark ridges on a light background) on each side (these will be the sts before the first marker (m) and after the second marker) and Basic Pattern 1 (light ridges on a dark background) across the center sts between the 2 markers. Cont inc 1 st at beg of every row, work patt as foll, shifting markers 3 sts away from the center every 4 rows as foll:

Row 129 (149): (RS) With L8, sl 1 kwise, M1, knit to last st, p1.

Row 130 (150): (WS) With L8, sl 1 kwise, M1, purl to first m, sl m, k2, sl m, purl to end of row.

Row 131 (151): (RS) With D, sl 1 kwise, M1, knit to last st, p1. Move each marker 3 sts away from center—8 sts between markers.

Row 132 (152): (WS) With D, sl 1 kwise, M1, knit to first m, sl m, p8, sl m, knit to last st, p1.

Row 133 (153): (RS) With L8, sl 1 kwise, M1, knit to last st, p1.

Row 134 (154): (WS) With L8, sl 1 kwise, M1, purl to first m, sl m, k8, sl m, purl to end of row.

Row 135 (155): (RS) With D, sl 1 kwise, M1, knit to last st, p1. Move each marker 3 sts away from center—14 sts between markers.

Row 136 (156): (WS) With D, sl 1 kwise, M1, knit to first m, sl m, p14, sl m, knit to last st, p1.

Row 137 (157): (RS) With L8, sl 1 kwise, M1, knit to last st, p1.

Row 138 (158): (WS) With L8, sl 1 kwise, M1, purl to first m, sl m, k14, sl m, purl to end of row.

Row 139 (159): (RS) With D, sl 1 kwise, M1, knit to last st, p1. Move each marker 3 sts away from center—20 sts between markers.

Row 140 (160): (WS) With D, sl 1 kwise, M1, knit to first m, sl m, p20, sl m, knit to last st, p1.

Row 141 (161): (RS) With L9, sl 1 kwise, M1, knit to last st, p1.

Row 142 (162): (WS) With L9, sl 1 kwise, M1, purl to first m, sl m, k20, sl m, purl to end of row.

Row 143 (163): (RS) With D, sl 1 kwise, M1, knit to last st, p1. Move each marker 3 sts away from center—26 sts between markers.

Row 144 (164): (WS) With D, sl 1 kwise, M1, knit to first m, sl m, p26, sl m, knit to last st, p1.

Row 145 (165): (RS) With L9, sl 1 kwise, M1, knit to last st, p1.

Row 146 (166): (WS) With L9, sl 1 kwise, M1, purl to first m, sl m, k26, sl m, purl to end of row.

Row 147 (167): (RS) With D, sl 1 kwise, M1, knit to last st, p1. Move each marker 3 sts away from center—32 sts between markers.

Row 148 (168): (WS) With D, sl 1 kwise, M1, knit to first m, sl m, p32, sl m, knit to last st, p1.

Cont both patts as established, changing light color every 20 rows, inc 1 st at beg of every row, moving each marker 3 more sts away from center every 4th row, and working center sts in Basic Pattern 1 (light ridges on a dark background) and sts outside markers in Basic Pattern 2 (dark ridges on a light background). The sleeve will be completed on Row 167 in D, and is worked in the second broad stripe of L8 for the smaller size and the first broad stripe of L9 for the larger size—144 (140) sts (the smaller size has 4 more sts than the larger).

Increase for left back and front

Row 168: (WS) With D, sl 1 kwise, work in patts to last st, k1 (do not purl last st).

Row 169: (RS) With D and using the knitted method (see Techniques, page 136), CO 88 (100) new sts for back—160 (170) sts to thread marker (woven through the rows from the sleeve cuff) at center of sleeve; thread marker represents shoulder line and division between back and front. On the same RS row, drop D, leaving it attached, and join L8 (L9) at the end of the new sts (new beg of row). With L8 (L9) and RS still facing, sl 1 kwise, work 9 sts in garter st (10 border sts; see Notes, page 88), pm, work to end of row as established, knitting last st instead of purling it.

Row 170: (WS) With L8 (L9) and using the knitted method, CO 88 (100) new sts for front—160 (170) sts to thread marker; 320 (340) sts total. With WS still facing and L8 (L9), sl 1 kwise, work 9 sts in garter st (10 border sts), pm, work to end as established.

Left back and front

Cont working 10 border sts at each end of needle, finish working the L8 (L9) broad stripe, then work broad stripes in the color order specified in Notes (page 88) until 3 ridges of L3 have been worked (for both sizes), ending with a WS row—270 (290) rows worked from beg of sleeve.

Left front neck

With RS facing, divide the work at the center thread marker—160 (170) sts on each side as foll: Thread about 30″ (76 cm) of waste cotton yarn on a tapestry needle and slip the first 160 (170) sts (for back) onto this yarn. Using the yarn as a stitch holder, tie the ends tog to secure the back sts until needed later. Cut yarns. With RS facing, join D and work front neck and neck edging as foll:

Row 1: (RS) With same cir needle, D, and working into the front st nearest the shoulder thread, use the knitted method to CO 10 sts for neck border—170 (180) front sts. With RS still facing, knit the new sts with D, pm, work to end as established.

Row 2: (WS) With D, sl 1 kwise, k9 (10-st border), sl m, work in established patt to next m, sl m, k9, p1 (10-st border).

Rows 3 and 4: With L3, work in established patts.

Dec row: (RS) With D, work 10 border sts (neck edging), sl m, sl 1 kwise, k2tog, pass slipped st over decreased st (double decrease), work to end as established—2 sts

decreased. Work 3 rows even in patt. Rep dec row every 4th row in this manner 5 more times (dec row is always worked in D on a RS row)—158 (168) sts rem. Cont even in patt, changing color sequence as established until 20 rows of L1 have been worked (5 ridges on RS).

Front edging

Work garter st for 15 rows as foll: *With L1, knit 2 rows. With D, knit 2 rows. Rep from * 2 more times, then knit 2 rows with L1, then knit 1 row (RS) with D. With WS facing and D, BO all sts kwise.

Left back neck

Place 160 (170) held back sts onto larger cir needle. With RS facing, join D at lower edge of back and work 1 row in patt (working from lower edge toward neck). *Next row:* (WS) Using the knitted method, CO 10 new sts for neck edging—170 (180) sts. With D and WS still facing, sl 1 kwise, k9 (border sts), pm, work in established patts to end of row. Work 2 rows with L3. *Dec row:* (RS row with D) Work to last 12 sts, k2tog, sl m, k9, p1 (border sts)—1 st decreased. Work 3 rows even in patt. Rep dec row every 4th row in this manner 5 more times—164 (174) sts rem. Cont even in patt, changing color sequence as established until the second stripe of L1 has been worked. Work 2 rows with D (center back). Place 164 (174) left back sts on waste yarn, ties ends of waste yarn tog to secure, and set aside.

RIGHT HALF OF JACKET

Work same as for the left side of jacket to end of sleeve.

Increase for right back and front

(WS) With D, sl 1 kwise, work in patt to last st, k1 (do not purl last st). At beg of next row (RS), use the knitted method to CO 88 (100) new sts for front—160 (170) sts to thread marker. Leave D attached and join L8 (L9) at end of new sts. With L8 (L9) and RS still facing, sl 1 kwise, work 9 sts in garter st (10 border sts), pm, work to end as established, knitting last st instead of purling it. At beg of next row (WS), use the knitted method to CO 88 (100) new sts for back—160 (170) sts to thread marker; 320 (340) sts total. With WS still facing and L8 (L9), sl 1 kwise, work 9 sts in garter st (10 border sts), pm, work to end as established.

Right back and front
Work as for left half of jacket.

Right back neck
With RS facing, divide the work at the center thread marker and secure first 160 (170) sts on waste yarn to work later for front. Cut yarns. *Next row:* (RS) Join D at back neck edge, and using the first st to the left of the center thread marker as the first st, use the knitted method to CO 10 new sts for back neck edging—170 (180) sts. With D and RS still facing, sl 1 kwise, k9 (border sts), pm, work in established patts to end of row. *Next row:* (WS) With D, work in patt. Work 2 rows with L3. *Dec row:* (RS row with D) Sl 1 kwise, k9 (border sts), sl m, ssk (see Techniques, page 137), work to last 10 sts, sl m, k9, p1 (border sts)—1 st decreased. Work 3 rows even in patt. Rep dec row every 4th row in this manner 5 more times—164 (174) sts rem. Cont even in patt, changing color sequence as established until the first row of the third ridge of L1 has been worked. Place 164 (174) right back sts on waste yarn, tie ends of waste yarn tog to secure, and set aside.

Right front neck
Place 160 (170) held front sts onto larger cir needle.
Row 1: With RS facing (working from lower edge toward neck), join D at lower edge of front, sl 1 kwise, k9, sl m, work in established patts to last st, k1.
Row 2: (WS) Using the knitted method, CO 10 new sts for neck edging—170 (180) sts. With D and WS still facing, sl 1 kwise, k9 (border sts), pm, work in established patts to end of row.
Rows 3 and 4: With L3, work in established patts.
Dec row: (RS) With D, work 10 border sts, sl m,

work in patt to last 13 sts, k3tog, sl m, work to end as established—2 sts decreased. Work 3 rows even in patt. Rep dec row every 4th row in this manner 5 more times (dec row is always worked in D on a RS row)—158 (168) sts rem. Cont even in patt, changing color sequence as established until 20 rows of L1 have been worked (5 ridges on RS).

Front edging
Work as for left half of jacket.

FINISHING

Transfer back sts from waste yarn and place onto two cir needles. With RS facing, L1 threaded on a tapestry needle, and using the Kitchener st (see Techniques, page 139), graft the two pieces tog along center back. Thread a tapestry needle with D for the sleeves and L8 (L9) to match the side edging, and sew sleeve and side seams. Sew neck edgings tog at shoulders. Block to measurements (see schematic below).

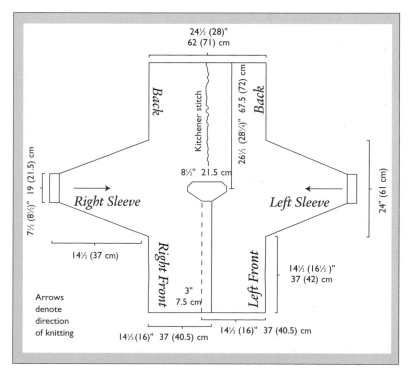

24½ (28)"
62 (71) cm

Back

Kitchener stitch

Back

26½ (28¼)" 67.5 (72) cm

8½" 21.5 cm

7½ (8½)" 19 (21.5) cm

24" (61 cm)

Right Sleeve

Left Sleeve

14½ (37 cm)

14½ (16½)"
37 (42) cm

Right Front

Left Front

Arrows denote direction of knitting

3"
7.5 cm

14½ (16)" 37 (40.5) cm

14½ (16)" 37 (40.5) cm

FINISHED SIZE

39 (40½, 42)" (99 [103, 106.5] cm). Vest shown measures 39" (99 cm).

YARN

Fingering-weight yarn. Vest requires about 434 (434, 651) yd (397 [397, 595] m) of dark yarn (D) and 217 (217, 434) yd (198 [198, 397] m) each of two light yarns (L1 and L2).

We suggest Harrisville Designs New England Shetland (100% pure virgin wool; 217 yd [198 m]/50 g): #33 midnight blue (D), 2 (2, 3) skeins; #13 peacock (L1) and #28 iris (L2), 1 (1, 2) skeins each.

NEEDLES

Size 1 (2.5 mm): 24" (60-cm) circular (cir) and set of 2 double-pointed (dpn). Adjust needle size if necessary to obtain the correct gauge.

NOTIONS

Markers (m); tapestry needle; safety pins or small stitch holders; seven ⅝" (1.5-cm) buttons; sewing needle and matching thread.

GAUGE

26 sts and 50 rows = 4" (10 cm) in zigzag pattern.

OCEAN VEST

....

This cropped vest is knit from side to side in three pieces using a zigzag shadow pattern.

NOTES

Before beginning, review Tips—Before You Knit, pages 11–14; Abbreviations, page 134; Techniques, pages 135–140.

This vest is worked sideways in three pieces. See page 96 for a schematic and knitting direction.

The charts for this vest are on pages 98–101. There is 1 edge stitch at each end of needle. Work the edge stitches as follows: Slip 1 knitwise at the beginning of every row, purl 1 at the end of every row. The edge stitches are included in the chart stitch count, but are not shown with specific edge stitch symbols in order not to disrupt the zigzag pattern.

Increases and decreases are worked 1 stitch in from the edge of the row (inside the edge stitches).

Instructions are given for the smallest size with the larger sizes in parentheses. If there is only one number, it applies to all sizes.

The yarns for this design can be purchased as a kit. See Resources, page 142 for more information.

LEFT FRONT

Front band

With D, dpn, and using the knitted method (see Techniques, page 136), CO 5 (7, 7) sts.

Row 1: (RS) Knit to last st, p1 (mark the RS with safety pin).

Row 2: (WS) Sl 1 kwise, knit to last st, p1. Rep Row 2 until there are 86 ridges on RS of work, then work WS row once more. Place 5 (7, 7) live sts on safety pin or stitch holder. Cut yarn, leaving a 4" (10-cm) tail. Cont as foll: *Set-up row 1:* With RS facing and cir needle, join D at outermost CO st. Pick up and knit sts along front band edging as foll: Working under both loops, pick up and knit 1 st in each edge st, end by picking up 1 st between the last picked-up st and the live st on holder—87 sts picked up.

Set-up row 2: (WS) With D, sl 1 kwise, k85, p1. Join L2 and work Left Front chart (page 98) as foll:

Row 1: (RS) With L2, sl 1 kwise, k85, p1.

Row 2: (WS) Sl 1 kwise, p22, k19, p22, k22, p1.

Row 3: With D, sl 1 kwise, k84, k1f&b, p1—88 sts.

Row 4: Sl 1 kwise, p1, [k20, p21] 2 times, k3, p1.

Cont as charted, changing colors as shown, and *at the same time* inc 1 st at the end of every RS row 20 times—107 sts. *Next row:* (Row 42 of chart) Using the knitted method, CO 13 (17, 21) sts. Beg with these new sts, work Row 42 of chart—120 (124, 128) sts.

Shape shoulder

Cont as charted, dec 1 st at shoulder edge (beg of WS rows; end of RS rows) on Row 53 (54, 56), then again on Row 65 (66, 70)—118 (122, 126) sts rem. Cont even through Row 73 (77, 81) of chart.

Shape armhole

At beg of WS Row 74 (78, 82), BO 12 (15, 18) sts—106 (107, 108) sts rem. At armhole edge, BO 4 sts 6 times, then BO 2 sts 5 (4, 4) times—72 (75, 76) sts rem. Dec 1 st at armhole edge every other row 4 (5, 4) times—68 (70, 72) sts rem. Work even in patt through Row 116 (122, 128) of chart. Using same yarn as for last row, BO all sts.

BACK

With D, (L1, D), CO 68 (70, 72) sts. Beg with Row 13 (7, 1), work Back, Left Half chart (page 99) through Row 25 (21, 19).

Shape left armhole

Beg with WS Row 26 (22, 20), use the knitted method to CO 1 st at armhole edge 4 (5, 4) times, then CO 2 sts 5 (4, 4) times, then CO 4 sts 6 times, ending with Row 55 (51, 47) of chart—106 (107, 108) sts. *Next row:* (WS) CO 12 (15, 18) sts, work to end of row—118 (122, 126) sts.

Shape left shoulder and neck

Cont as charted, CO 1 st at armhole edge on Row 68 (64, 60), then again on Row 78 (76, 74)—120 (124, 128) sts. Cont even through Row 87 of chart. *Next row:* (WS Row 88) BO 2 sts, work to end—118 (122, 126) sts rem. BO 1 st at neck edge (beg of WS rows) 8 times—110 (114, 118) sts rem. Cont in patt through Row 130 of chart. Do not BO. With L1 and beg with Row 131, work Back, Right Half chart (page 100) through Row 155.

Shape right neck and shoulder

Beg with WS Row 156, CO 1 st at neck edge 8 times—118 (122, 126) sts. CO 2 sts at beg of Row 172—120 (124, 128) sts. Cont as charted, BO 1 st at shoulder edge on Row 182 (184, 186), then again on Row 194 (196, 200)—118 (122, 126) sts. Cont even through Row 203 (207, 211).

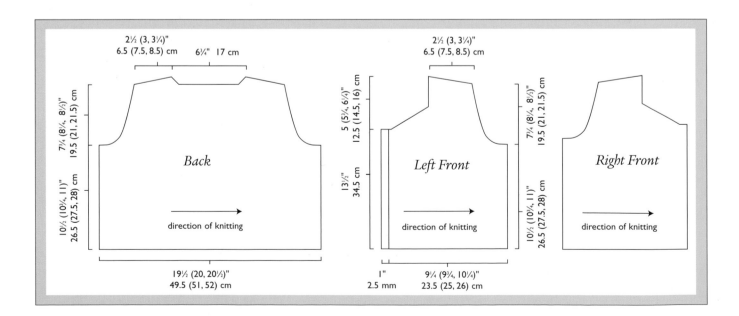

Shape right armhole

At beg of WS Row 204 (208, 212), BO 12 (15, 18) sts—106 (107, 108) sts rem. At armhole edge, BO 4 sts 6 times, then BO 2 sts 5 (4, 4) times, then BO 1 st 4 (5, 4) times—68 (70, 72) sts rem. Work through Row 246 (252, 258) of chart. Using same yarn as for last row worked, BO all sts.

Right Front

With D (L2, D), CO 68 (70, 72) sts. Beg with Row 13 (7, 1), work Right Front chart (page 101) through Row 25 (21, 19).

Shape armhole

Beg with WS Row 26 (22, 20), use the knitted method to CO 1 st at armhole edge 4 (5, 4) times, then CO 2 sts 5 (4, 4) times, then CO 4 sts 6 times, then CO 12 (15, 18) sts once—118 (122, 126) sts.

Shape shoulder

Cont as charted, CO 1 st at armhole edge on Row 66 (64, 60), then again on Row 78 (76, 74)—120 (124, 128) sts. Cont even through Row 87 of chart.

Shape neck

(WS Row 88) BO 13 (17, 21) sts—107 sts rem. BO 1 st at neck edge 20 times—87 sts rem. Work through Row 130, ending by working 2 rows in D. Do not BO.

FINISHING

Right front band: With D, dpn, and using the knitted method beg with the lowest st, CO 5 (7, 7) sts.

Row 1: (RS) K4 (6, 6), p2tog (1 band st and 1 body st), turn.

Row 2: (WS) Sl 1 kwise, k3 (5, 5), p1, turn.

Row 3: (RS) Sl 1 kwise, k3 (5, 5), p3tog (1 band st and 2 body sts), turn.

Row 4: (WS) Sl 1 kwise, k3 (5, 5), p1, turn.

Row 5: (RS) Sl 1 kwise, k3 (5, 5), p2tog, turn.

Row 6: Rep Row 4—3 garter ridges on RS of work.

Row 7: (Buttonhole row) Sl 1 kwise, k0 (2, 2), k2tog, yo twice, k1 (2, 2) through the back loop (tbl) to twist the st(s), p2tog, turn.

Row 8: Rep Row 4, working k1 into first loop of double yo of previous row and dropping the extra loop from the needle.

*Rep Rows 5 and 4 until there are 13 garter ridges on RS, then rep Row 7 for buttonhole; rep from * for a total of 6 buttonholes (the 7th buttonhole will be worked in the neck border), then rep Rows 4 and 5 until 3 body sts rem. Work Row 3 once, then work Rows 4, 5, and 4. Do not BO. With yarn still attached, slip border sts onto safety pin or stitch holder.

Shoulder seams: With RS tog and matching stripe colors, use yarn threaded on a tapestry needle to sew shoulder seams.

Neck edging: Slip held right front border sts onto cir needle. With D still attached to sts and RS facing, work border sts as sl 1 kwise, k4 (6, 6), then pick up and knit 38 (40, 42) sts across right front neckline to right front shoulder seam, 45 (47, 49) sts across back neck to second shoulder seam, 38 (40, 42) sts across left front neckline, then work the held left front border sts as k4 (6, 6), p1—131 (141, 151) sts total. Knit 1 WS row, working k2tog at each corner of front neck edge and working k2tog at each corner of back neck. *Next row:* (RS) Work buttonhole same as Row 7 of front band, then knit to end of row. Knit 2 more rows, working 1 edge st at each side of center fronts. With WS facing, BO all sts kwise.

Armhole edging: With D and cir needle, pick up and knit 126 (130, 134) sts evenly spaced around armhole. Knit 4 rows. With WS facing, BO all sts kwise.

With yarn threaded on a tapestry needle, sew side seams, working 1 row in from side edges so that there will be 2 rows of the same color at each seam (1 row from each side of seam). Sew buttons to left front band, opposite buttonholes. Weave in loose ends to WS and secure.

Left Front

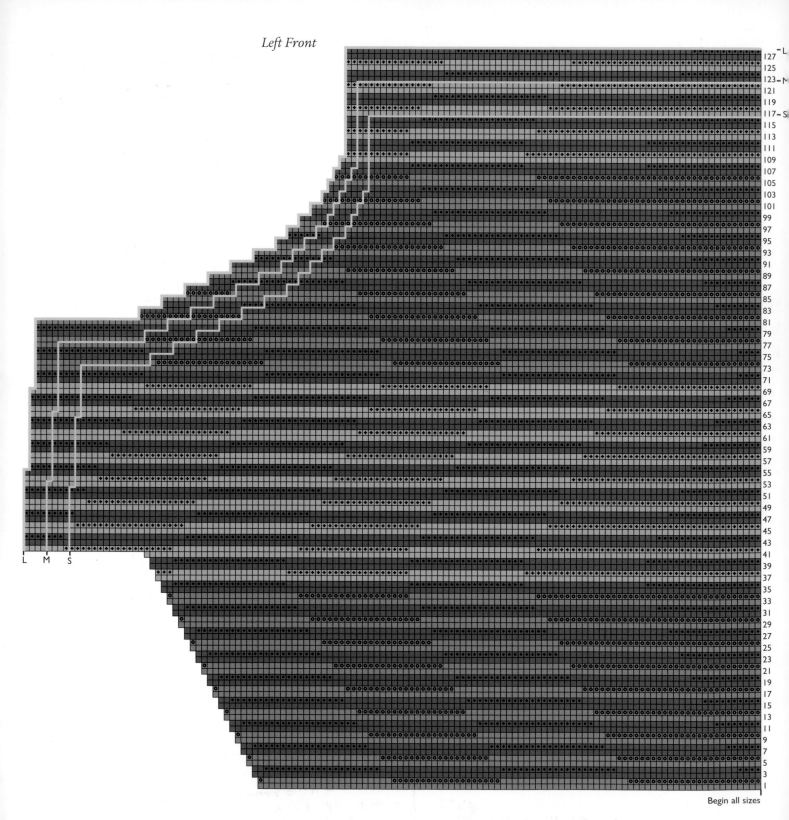

Begin all sizes

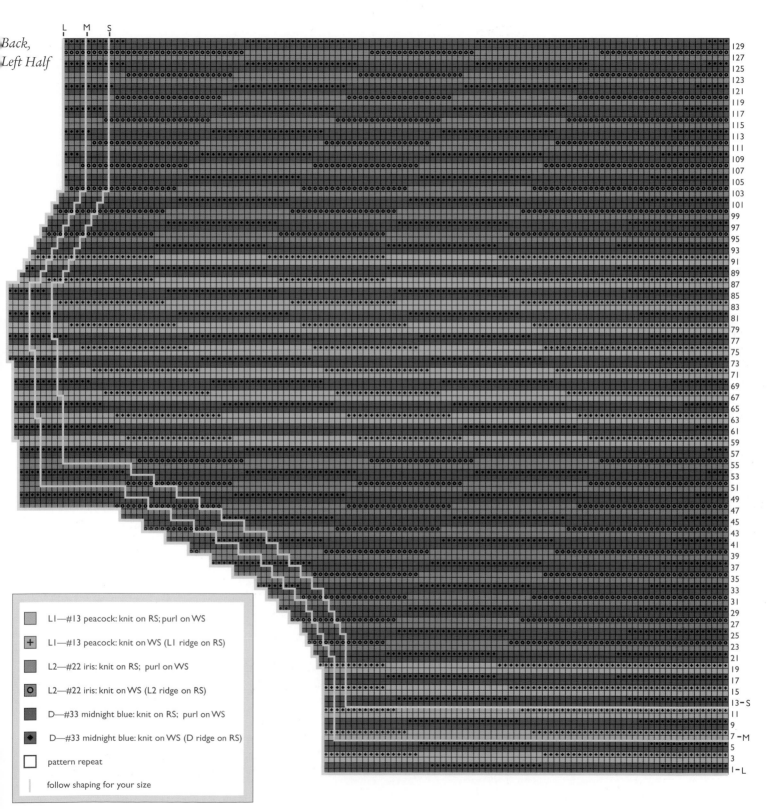

Back, Left Half

L M S

129
127
125
123
121
119
117
115
113
111
109
107
105
103
101
99
97
95
93
91
89
87
85
83
81
79
77
75
73
71
69
67
65
63
61
59
57
55
53
51
49
47
45
43
41
39
37
35
33
31
29
27
25
23
21
19
17
15
13-S
11
9
7-M
5
3
1-L

Legend:

	L1—#13 peacock: knit on RS; purl on WS
+	L1—#13 peacock: knit on WS (L1 ridge on RS)
	L2—#22 iris: knit on RS; purl on WS
⊙	L2—#22 iris: knit on WS (L2 ridge on RS)
	D—#33 midnight blue: knit on RS; purl on WS
◆	D—#33 midnight blue: knit on WS (D ridge on RS)
☐	pattern repeat
│	follow shaping for your size

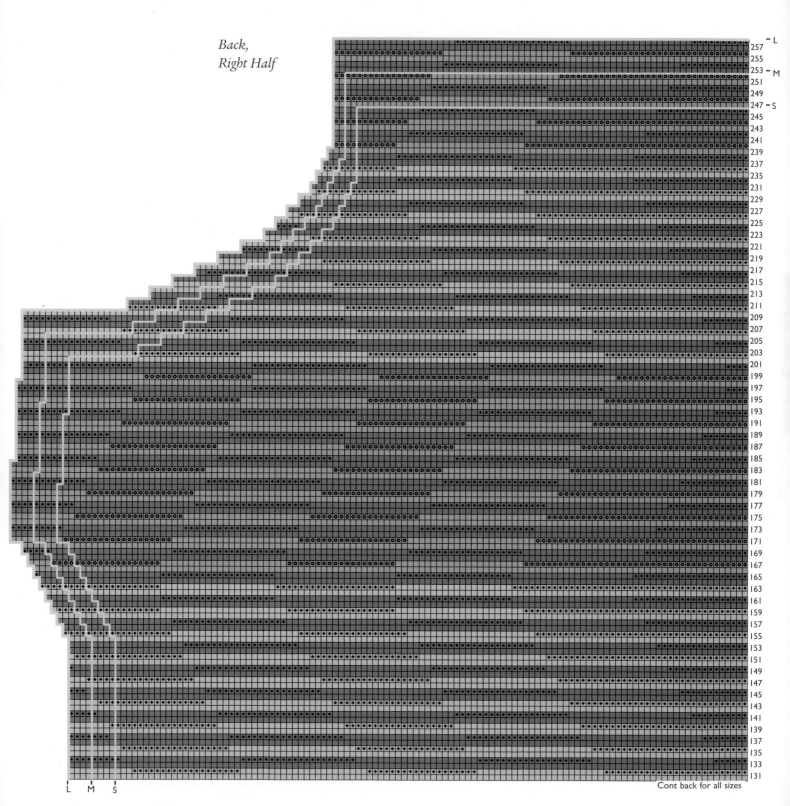

*Back,
Right Half*

Cont back for all sizes

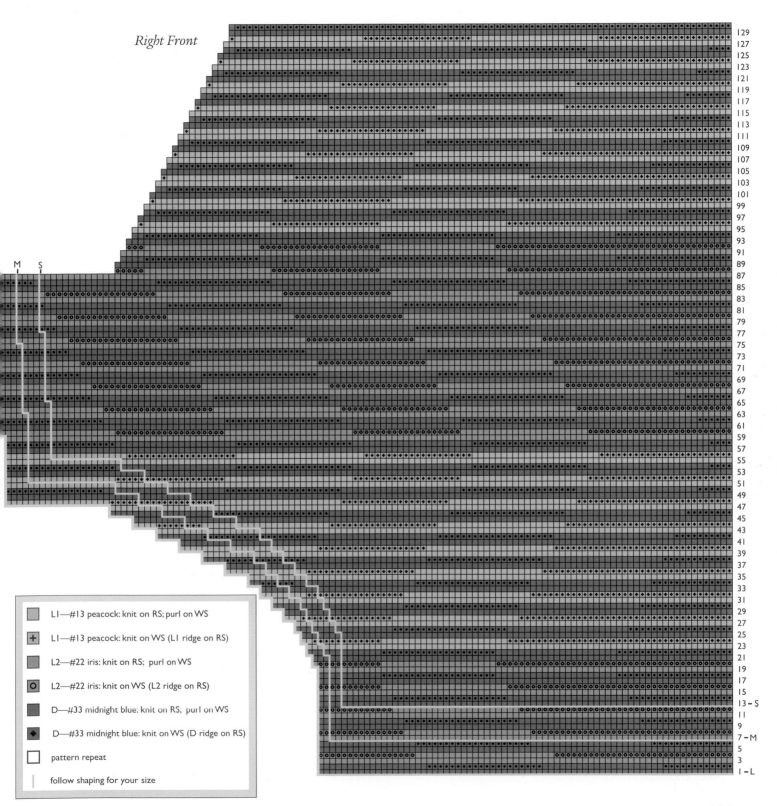

Right Front

Legend:
- L1—#13 peacock: knit on RS; purl on WS
- + L1—#13 peacock: knit on WS (L1 ridge on RS)
- L2—#22 iris: knit on RS; purl on WS
- ○ L2—#22 iris: knit on WS (L2 ridge on RS)
- D—#33 midnight blue: knit on RS; purl on WS
- ◆ D—#33 midnight blue: knit on WS (D ridge on RS)
- □ pattern repeat
- | follow shaping for your size

Row numbers (right side): 1 – L, 3, 5, 7 – M, 9, 11, 13 – S, 15, 17, 19, 21, 23, 25, 27, 29, 31, 33, 35, 37, 39, 41, 43, 45, 47, 49, 51, 53, 55, 57, 59, 61, 63, 65, 67, 69, 71, 73, 75, 77, 79, 81, 83, 85, 87, 89, 91, 93, 95, 97, 99, 101, 103, 105, 107, 109, 111, 113, 115, 117, 119, 121, 123, 125, 127, 129

FINISHED SIZE

40" (101.5 cm) chest/bust circumference.

YARN

Sport-weight yarn. Top requires about 510 yd (466 m) dark yarn (D) and 340 yd (310 m) each of two light yarns (L1 and L2). We suggest Rowan 4-ply Cotton (100% cotton; 187 yd [170 m]/50 g): #101 black (D), 3 balls; #127 flirty (pink; L1) and #134 zest (yellow; L2), 2 balls each.

NEEDLES

US Size 1 (2.25 mm): straight, 16" and 24" (40-cm and 60-cm) circular (cir), and 1 double-pointed (dpn). Adjust needle size if necessary to obtain the correct gauge.

NOTIONS

Markers (m); tapestry needle.

GAUGE

27 sts and 50 rows = 4" (10 cm) in charted pattern.

TRIANGLE TOP

....

This simple, lightweight summer top is knit sideways in two pieces—the back and the front.

NOTES

Before beginning, review Tips—Before You Knit, pages 11–14; Abbreviations, page 134; Techniques, pages 135–140.

The charts for this top are on pages 106, 107, 108, and 109. There is one edge stitch at each end of needle that is not shown on charts. Work the edge stitches as follows: Slip 1 knitwise at the beginning of every row, purl 1 at the end of every row.

The schematic for this top is on page 104. The back is worked sideways from right side seam to left side seam, with armholes, shoulders, and neck shaped along the way. The front is worked from left side seam to right side seam, also with armholes, shoulders, and neck shaped along the way.

BACK

Right side edge

With D, 24" (60-cm) cir needle, and using the knitted method (see Techniques, page 136) CO 72 sts. Sl 1 kwise (edge st; not shown on chart), work next 70 sts according to Row 1 of Right Back chart (page 106; note that 17 sts inside rep frame are

worked 4 times), p1 (edge st; not shown on chart). Working 1 edge st each end of needle as established (see Notes), work rem 70 sts through Row 10 of chart.

Shape right armhole

(RS Row 11) Sl 1 kwise (edge st), M1 (see Techniques, page 138), work as established to end—1 st increased. Work 1 WS row even in patt. Inc 1 st at beg of every RS row in this manner 4 more times—77 sts (including edge sts). *Next RS row:* (Row 21) Using the knitted method, CO 2 sts at beg of row; beg with these new sts, cont in patt to end of row—2 sts increased. Work 1 WS row even in patt. CO 2 sts at beg of every RS row in this manner 3 more times—85 sts. *Next RS row:* (Row 29) Using the knitted method, CO 4 sts at beg of row; beg with these new sts, cont in patt to end of row—4 sts increased. Work 1 WS row even in patt. CO 4 sts at beg of every RS row in this manner 5 more times—109 sts. *Next RS row:* (Row 41) Using the knitted method, CO 15 sts—124 sts.

Shape right shoulder

Cont on 124 sts through Row 52 of chart. Inc 1 st at beg of next row, then work 11

rows even. Rep the last 12 rows once more, ending with Row 76 of chart—126 sts.

Shape right neck

Next RS row: (Row 77) BO 2 sts, work in patt to end—124 sts rem. Beg with Row 79 of chart, dec 1 st at beg of every RS row 8 times as foll: Sl 1 kwise (edge st), ssk (see Techniques, page 137), work in patt to end. Work WS rows even in patt. When all decs have been completed, there will rem 116 sts and Row 93 will have been completed. Cont even through end of Right Back chart (Row 126). Do not BO.

Shape left neck

Maintaining 1 edge st each end of needle as established, work center 114 sts according to Rows 1–34 of Left Back chart (page 107). Beg with Row 35, inc 1 st at beg of every RS row 8 times as foll: Sl 1 kwise (edge st), M1, work in patt to end—124 sts (including edge sts). *Next RS row:* (Row 51) Use the knitted method to CO 2 sts at beg of row, work in patt to end—126 sts.

Shape left shoulder

Cont even on 126 sts through Row 62. Dec 1 st at beg of next row, then work 11 rows even. Rep the last 12 rows once more, ending with Row 86—124 sts rem.

Shape left armhole

(Row 87) BO 15 sts, work to end in patt—109 sts rem. Cont in patt and beg with Row 89, BO 4 sts at beg of next 6 RS rows—85 sts rem. Beg with Row 101, BO 2 sts at beg of next 4 RS rows—77 sts rem. Beg with Row 109, dec 1 st at beg of next 5 RS rows as foll: Sl 1 kwise (edge st), ssk, work in patt to end—72 sts rem. Work even through end of Left Back chart (Row 126). With D, BO all sts.

FRONT

Left side edge

With D, 24" (60-cm) cir needle, and using the knitted method, CO 72 sts. Working 1 edge st each end of

needle as for back (edge sts are not shown on charts), work center 70 sts according to Left Front chart (page 108) for 10 rows.

Shape left armhole

Beg with next row (Row 11), inc 1 st at beg of row every RS row 5 times as for right back armhole—77 sts (including edge sts). Cont working 1 edge st each end of needle and foll Left Front chart, use the knitted method to CO 2 sts at beg of next 4 RS rows—85 sts. Beg with Row 29 of chart, CO 4 sts at beg of next 6 RS rows—109 sts. At beg of next row (Row 41), CO 15 sts—124 sts.

Shape left shoulder

Cont even on 124 sts through Row 52 of chart. Inc 1 st at beg of next row, then work 11 rows even. Rep the last 12 rows once more, ending with Row 76 of chart—126 sts.

Shape left neck

Next RS row: (Row 77) BO 4 sts, work in patt to end—122 sts rem. Beg with Row 79, BO 9 sts at beg of next 2 RS rows—104 sts rem. Beg with Row 83, BO 2 sts at beg of next 7 RS rows—90 sts rem. Work 3 rows even. BO 2 sts at beg of next row (Row 99)—88 sts rem. Work 5 rows even. BO 2 sts at beg of next row (Row 105)—86 sts rem. Work 7 rows even. BO 2 sts at beg of next row (Row 113)—84 sts

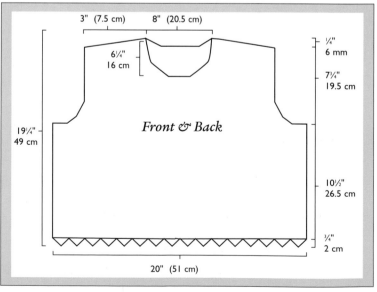

rem. Cont even through end of Left Front chart (Row 126). Do not BO.

Shape right neck

Maintaining 1 edge st each end of needle as established, work center 82 sts according to Rows 1–14 of Right Front chart (page 109). Using the knitted method, CO 2 sts at beg of next row (Row 15)—86 sts. Work 7 rows even in patt. CO 2 sts at beg of next row (Row 23)—88 sts. Work 5 rows even. CO 2 sts at beg of next row (Row 29)—90 sts. Work 3 rows even. Beg with Row 33, CO 2 sts at beg of every RS row 7 times—104 sts. Beg with Row 47, CO 9 sts at beg of next 2 RS rows—122 sts. CO 4 sts at beg of next RS row (Row 51)—126 sts.

Shape right shoulder

Cont even on 126 sts through Row 62 of chart. Dec 1 st at beg of next row, then work 11 rows even. Rep the last 12 rows once more, ending with Row 86 of chart—124 sts rem.

Shape right armhole

(Row 87) BO 15 sts, work to end in patt—109 sts rem. Cont in patt, beg with Row 89, BO 4 sts at beg of next 6 RS rows—85 sts rem. Beg with Row 101, BO 2 sts at beg of next 4 RS rows—77 sts rem. Beg with Row 109, dec 1 st at beg of next 5 RS rows as foll: Sl 1 kwise (edge st), ssk, work in patt to end—72 sts rem. Work even through end of Right Front chart (Row 126). With D, BO all sts.

FINISHING

Seams: With RS of front and back facing each other, use D threaded on a tapestry needle and the mattress st (see Techniques, page 140) to sew front to back at shoulders, matching D stripes (most L1 stripes will meet L2 stripes). Sew side seams. Weave in loose ends to WS of work.

Neck edging: With D, 16″ or 24″ (40-cm or 60-cm) cir needle, and RS facing, pick up and knit 55 sts across back neck and 100 sts around front neck—155 sts total. Join into a rnd. Knit 8 rnds. BO all sts loosely. Fold edging in half to WS and pin in place. With D and using a whipstitch (see Techniques, page 140), sew BO row to WS of neck opening. Remove pins.

Armhole edgings: With D, 24″ (60-cm) cir needle, RS facing, and beg at underarm seam, pick up and knit 60 sts from underarm to shoulder seam, then pick up and knit 60 sts from shoulder to underarm seam—120 sts total. Join into a rnd. Knit 8 rnds. BO all sts loosely. Fold edging in half to WS and pin in place. With D and using a whipstitch, sew BO row to WS of armhole. Remove pins.

Lower edging: (*Note:* The two colors at each side seam are not full patt reps, so fewer sts are picked up in these areas. The partial side reps will each have two sawtooth triangles; the full reps will have three triangles.)
With D, 24″ (60-cm) cir needle, RS facing, and beg at right front side seam, *pick up and knit 12 sts across first partial rep, then pick up and knit 18 sts across each of the next 6 full reps, pick up and knit 12 sts across next partial rep; rep from * across back—264 sts total. Join into a rnd. Purl 1 rnd (forms a ridge on RS). Working 6 sts at a time with dpn, work sawtooth edging as foll, using L1 along the L1 pattern areas and L2 along the L2 pattern areas:
Row 1: (RS) K2, turn.
Row 2: K1, p1, turn.
Row 3: Sl 1 kwise with yarn in back (wyb), k2, turn.
Row 4: K2, p1, turn.
Row 5: Sl 1 kwise wyb, k3, turn.
Row 6: K3, p1, turn.
Row 7: Sl 1 kwise wyb, k4, turn.
Row 8: K4, p1, turn.
Row 9: Sl 1 kwise, k5, turn.
Row 10: K5, p1, turn.
Row 11: (RS) BO 6 sts (1 st rem on dpn), k1 from cir needle, turn.
Rep Rows 2–11 until all sts have been used, changing colors as necessary. On last rep, cut yarn, pull tail through rem st, and fasten off.

Weave in loose ends. Block to measurements (see schematic, page 104).

Right Back

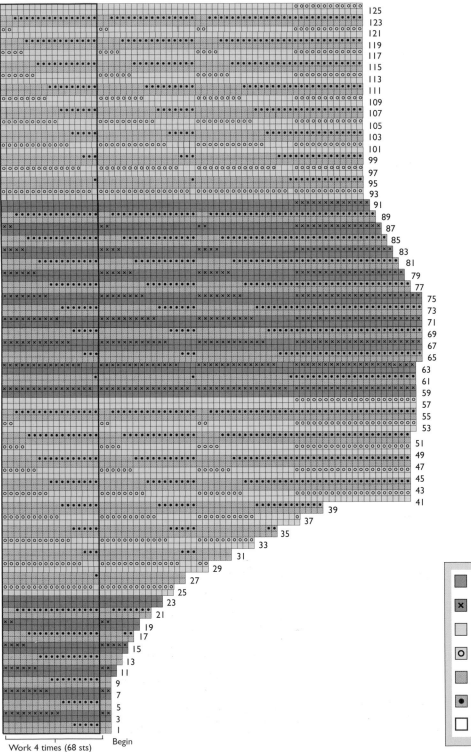

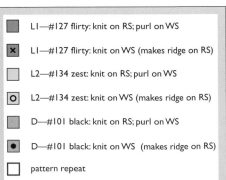

	L1—#127 flirty: knit on RS; purl on WS
	L1—#127 flirty: knit on WS (makes ridge on RS)
	L2—#134 zest: knit on RS; purl on WS
	L2—#134 zest: knit on WS (makes ridge on RS)
	D—#101 black: knit on RS; purl on WS
	D—#101 black: knit on WS (makes ridge on RS)
	pattern repeat

Work 4 times (68 sts)

Begin

Left Back

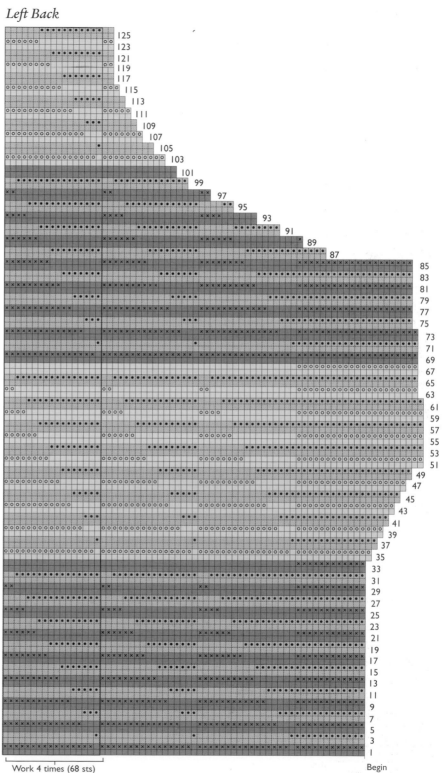

125
123
121
119
117
115
113
111
109
107
105
103
101
99
97
95
93
91
89
87
85
83
81
79
77
75
73
71
69
67
65
63
61
59
57
55
53
51
49
47
45
43
41
39
37
35
33
31
29
27
25
23
21
19
17
15
13
11
9
7
5
3
1

Work 4 times (68 sts)

Begin

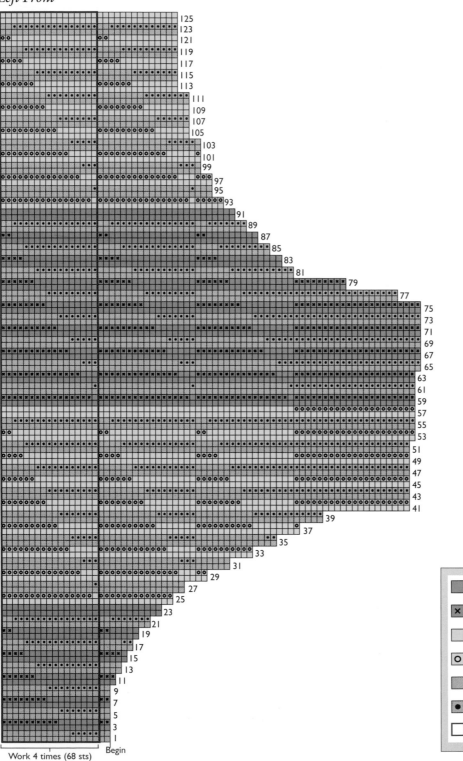

125
123
121
119
117
115
113
111
109
107
105
103
101
99
97
95
93
91
89
87
85
83
81
79
77
75
73
71
69
67
65
63
61
59
57
55
53
51
49
47
45
43
41
39
37
35
33
31
29
27
25
23
21
19
17
15
13
11
9
7
5
3
1

Begin

Work 4 times (68 sts)

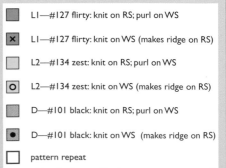

■	L1—#127 flirty: knit on RS; purl on WS
✕	L1—#127 flirty: knit on WS (makes ridge on RS)
▨	L2—#134 zest: knit on RS; purl on WS
⊙	L2—#134 zest: knit on WS (makes ridge on RS)
▨	D—#101 black: knit on RS; purl on WS
●	D—#101 black: knit on WS (makes ridge on RS)
□	pattern repeat

Right Front

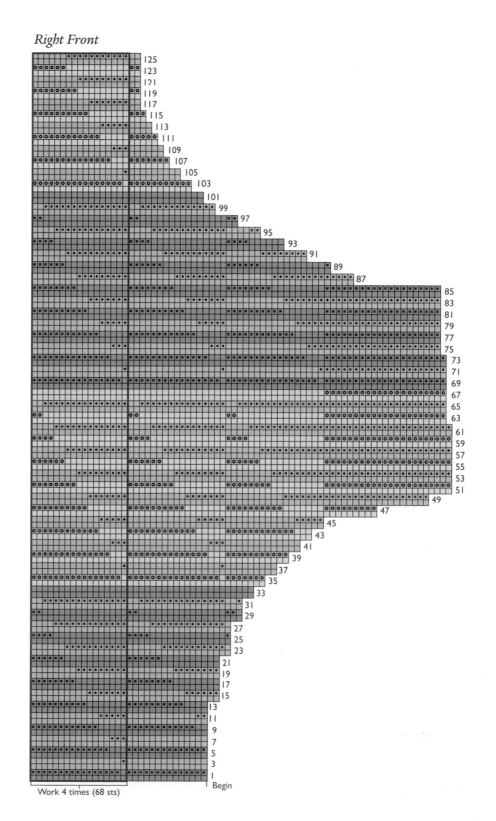

Work 4 times (68 sts)

Begin

FINISHED SIZE

53" (134.5 cm) chest/bust circumference.

YARN

Fingering-weight yarn. Jacket requires about 1500 yd (1371 m) dark yarn (D) and about 650 yd (590 m) each of two light yarns (L1 and L2).

We suggest Harrisville Designs New England Shetland (100% pure virgin wool; 217 yd [198 m]/50 g). Colorway #1 (shown on page 111): #33 midnight blue (D), 7 skeins; #84 lime (L1) and #83 grass (L2), 3 skeins each. Colorway #2 (shown on page 119): #50 black (D), 7 skeins; #46 oatmeal (L1) and #42 camel (L2), 3 skeins each.

NEEDLES

US size 2 (3 mm): 24" or 32" (60-cm or 80-cm) circular (cir). US size 1 (2.5 mm): 16" (40-cm) cir, and 2 double-pointed (dpn) for collar and edgings. 2 spare size 1 or 2 (2.5-mm or 3-mm) cir needles for holding sts during three-needle BO. Adjust needle size if necessary to obtain the correct gauge.

COLLARED JACKET

·················

Knit from side to side, this oversized jacket features a unique border with a double-knitted front edge, and a large, cozy collar.

NOTES

Before beginning, review Tips—Before You Knit, pages 11–14; Abbreviations, page 134; Techniques, pages 135–140.

The charts for this project are on pages 112, 115, 116, and 117. There is one edge stitch each side of each piece. Edge stitches are not shown on charts. Work edge stitches as follows: Slip 1 knitwise at beginning of every row; purl 1 at end of every row.

Charts are shown in Colorway #2 colors; see Yarn at left for Colorway #1 colors.

A schematic of this project is on page 118. The body pieces are worked sideways. The back is worked from left side edge to right side edge, with the neck shaped along the way. The right front is worked from right side edge to center front; the left front is worked from center front to left side edge. The sleeves are worked from shoulders to cuffs.

The color sequence shifts from L2 at the back left side edge to L1 at the back right side edge. The right front begins with L1 at the side edge and shifts to L2 at the center front. The left front begins with L1 and ends with L2 at the side edge. The sleeves pick up the color pattern following the right and left sides. The zigzag pattern and the colors align at the shoulders.

Although the knitted cast-on is usually worked as a permanent cast-on, in this project it is worked with waste cotton yarn that is later removed (making it a provisional, or temporary, cast-on).

The yarn for these two jackets can be purchased as kits. See Resources, page 142 for more information.

BACK

With larger cir needle, waste cotton yarn, and using the knitted method (see Techniques, page 136), temporarily CO 162 sts—160 back sts plus 1 edge st each side. Join L2 and work as foll: Sl 1 kwise (edge st; not shown on chart), k160 sts according to Row 1 (RS) of Left Back chart (page 112), p1 (edge st; not shown on chart). Working edge sts as described in Notes, work center 160 sts through Row 107 of chart (*Note:* Rows 1–76 are on one chart; Rows 77–152 are on a second chart).

Colorway #1

NOTIONS

About 3 yd (2.74 m) smooth waste cotton yarn to use as stitch holders and for provisional (temporary) cast-on; markers (m); tapestry needle; nine ¾" (2-cm) buttons; sharp-point sewing needle and thread to match buttons.

GAUGE

24 sts and 46 rows = 4" (10 cm) in charted pattern on size 2 (3 mm) needles.

Shape neck

(*Note:* Neck shaping is indicated by green line on chart and is worked on last 6 sts on needle; i.e., follow neck shaping on last widthwise rep of chart.)

Row 108: (WS) BO 4 sts, work in patt to end—158 sts rem. Cont in patt as established, re-establish edge st at neck edge and dec 1 st at beg of needle on Rows 110 and 114—156 sts rem. Cont even in patt through Row 152 of chart. Change to Right Back chart (page 115) and L2 and D. The zigzag patt shifts in the opposite direction for the second half of the back. Cont working 1 edge st each side and cont to foll green line for neck shaping, work on 156 sts through Row 38 of chart.

Next row: (Row 39 of chart) Work to last st, M1 (see Techniques, page 138), p1 (edge st)—157 sts. Work 3 rows even. Inc 1 st at end of next row—158 sts. Work 1 WS row even.

Left Back, Rows 1–76

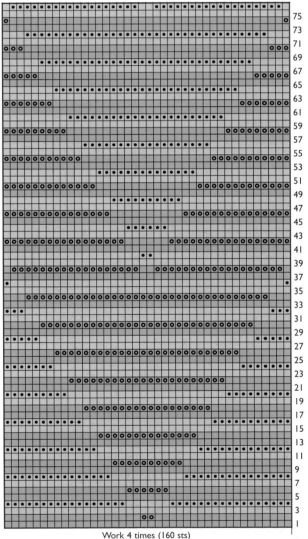

Work 4 times (160 sts)

Begin

Left Back, Rows 77–152

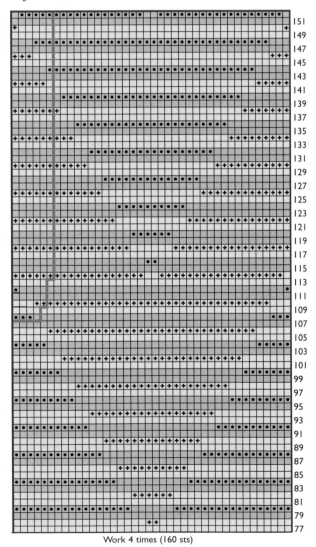

Work 4 times (160 sts)

Next row: (Row 45 of chart) Work all sts, then with RS still facing, use the backward loop method (see Techniques, page 135) to CO 4 sts—162 sts.

Cont working 1 edge st each end of needle, work through Row 152 of chart. Place all sts on waste yarn holder.

RIGHT FRONT

The right front is worked from side edge to center front. With waste yarn, larger cir needle, and using the knitted method, CO 162 sts—160 front sts plus 1 edge st each side. Change to L1 and working 1 edge st each end of needle as for back, work center 160 sts and colors according to Rows 1–107 of Right Front chart (page 116).

Shape neck

(*Note:* Neck shaping is indicated by green line on chart and is worked on last 40 sts on needle; i.e., follow neck shaping on last widthwise rep of chart.) At beg of next WS row (Row 108), BO 10 sts, work to end—152 sts rem. Work 1 RS row even. At beg of next WS row (Row 110), BO 10 sts, work to end—142 sts rem. Working 1 edge st each side as established, work 2 rows even. Beg with next RS row (Row 113), dec 1 st at neck edge every RS row 20 times as foll: Work to last 3 sts, k2tog, p1 (edge st)—122 sts rem. Work even through Row 152 of chart. Place all sts on waste yarn holder.

LEFT FRONT

The left front is worked from center front to side edge.

With waste yarn, larger cir needle, and using the knitted method, CO 122 sts—120 front sts plus 1 edge st each side. With L1 and beg with Row 1, work Left Front chart (page 117), and *at the same time* foll green line for neck shaping on Rows 1–45 as foll: Beg with Row 3, inc 1 st at end of every RS row 20 times as foll: Sl 1 kwise (edge st), M1, work in patt to end—142 sts after Row 41 has been worked. At beg of next 2 RS rows, use the backward loop method to CO 10 sts—162 sts. Cont even in patt through Row 152 of chart. Place all sts on waste yarn holder.

SLEEVES

With yarn threaded on a tapestry needle and using the mattress stitch, sew fronts to back at shoulders.

Right sleeve

Remove waste yarn from CO edge of right front, and *at the same time* carefully place the lower 101 live sts on another length of waste yarn, place marker (pm), and place the rem 61 live sts onto larger cir needle. Cont along right back, remove waste yarn from back CO edge, and place first 61 live sts onto same cir needle, pm, place rem 101 sts onto another length of waste yarn—122 live sts on cir needle to work for sleeve; 101 sts each on yarn holders for front and back side edge. Tie the ends of the waste yarn tog to secure rem sts. Turn work so jacket body is closest to you, and with RS facing, join L2 at beg of back sleeve sts. Beg with Row 1, work through Row 152 of Left Back chart (page

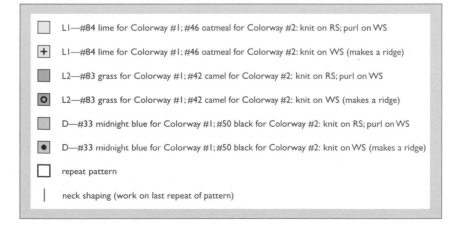

112), then work Rows 1–38, ending with 2 rows L2—190 rows total; piece should measure about 16½" (42 cm) from beg. *At the same time,* shape sleeve as foll: Work 4 rows even, then on the next row, and every 6th row thereafter, dec 1 st each end of needle 31 times as foll: Sl 1 kwise (edge st), ssk (see Techniques, page 137), knit to last 3 sts, ssk, p1 (edge st)—2 sts decreased per dec row; 60 sts rem after 62 rows have been worked. Do not BO. Place all sts on waste yarn holder.

Left sleeve

Remove waste yarn from BO edge of back, and *at the same time* carefully place the lower 101 live sts on another length of waste yarn, pm, and place the next 61 live sts onto larger cir needle. Cont along left front, remove waste yarn from front CO edge, and place first 61 sts onto same cir needle, pm, place rem 101 sts on waste yarn—122 live sts on cir needle for sleeve; 101 sts each on yarn holders. Tie ends of yarn holders to secure sts. Work as for right sleeve, but follow Right Front chart (page 116). Do not BO sts.

FRONT BORDERS AND COLLAR

The unique border on this jacket is essentially k2, p2 ribbing with a double-knitted front edge. The border continues up into the collar, which is ribbed in a continuation of the edging. Stitches are picked up from around the neck edge and the two neckbands are worked separately, then joined by knitting together to produce a double-sided neckband with smooth knit sts on both sides.

Right front band

Remove waste yarn from 122 center right front sts, and beg at the neck edge, place the sts onto smaller cir needle. Mark position of 7 buttonholes as foll: One at the point of each zigzag, and one halfway between each zigzag. With D, dpn, and beg with lowest st at bottom of jacket, use the knitted method to CO 7 sts for front band. Work as foll:

Row 1: (RS) Work k1f&b in each of the first 2 sts, p2, k2, p2tog (1 new st and 1 center front st)—9 sts. Turn work.

Row 2: (WS) Sl 1 kwise, p2, k2, [sl 1 pwise with yarn in front (wyf), k1] 2 times.

Row 3: (RS) [Sl 1 pwise wyf, k1] 2 times, p2, k2, p2tog, turn.

Row 4: (WS) Sl 1 kwise, p2, k2, [sl 1 pwise wyf, k1] 2 times.

Row 5: (RS; buttonhole row) [Sl 1 pwise wyf, k1] 2 times, BO 2 sts for buttonhole, k1, p2tog, turn.

Row 6: (WS) Sl 1 kwise, p2, turn work and use the knitted method to CO 2 sts to complete buttonhole, turn again, [sl 1 pwise wyf, k1] 2 times.

Rep Rows 3–4 to position of next buttonhole, then work Rows 5 and 6 for each buttonhole—7 buttonholes along right front; 2 more buttonholes will be worked in collar. Rep Rows 3 and 4 until all front edge sts have been worked, ending with Row 4—9 front band sts rem.

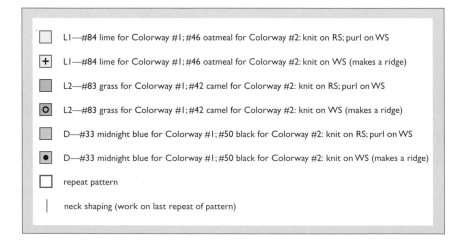

L1—#84 lime for Colorway #1; #46 oatmeal for Colorway #2: knit on RS; purl on WS

L1—#84 lime for Colorway #1; #46 oatmeal for Colorway #2: knit on WS (makes a ridge)

L2—#83 grass for Colorway #1; #42 camel for Colorway #2: knit on RS; purl on WS

L2—#83 grass for Colorway #1; #42 camel for Colorway #2: knit on WS (makes a ridge)

D—#33 midnight blue for Colorway #1; #50 black for Colorway #2: knit on RS; purl on WS

D—#33 midnight blue for Colorway #1; #50 black for Colorway #2: knit on WS (makes a ridge)

repeat pattern

neck shaping (work on last repeat of pattern)

Outside neckband

(RS) Work Row 3 as foll: [Sl 1 pwise wyf, k1] 2 times, p2, k2 (these 8 sts will form the front band from this point on), with smaller cir needle, knit the 9th st of front band as the first st of neckband, then pick up and knit 52 more sts along front neck edge to right shoulder seam, 1 st in shoulder seam, 54 sts across back neck, 1 st in left shoulder seam, and 53 sts to left center front edge—170 sts total; 8 front band sts and 162 outside neckband sts. Leave sts on needle (or place on holder) and set aside.

Left front band

Remove waste yarn from 122 held left front sts, and working from neck to lower body, place these sts onto smaller cir needle. Turn work so WS is facing, join D at the lower edge, and with dpn and using the knitted method, CO 7

Right Back, Rows 1–76

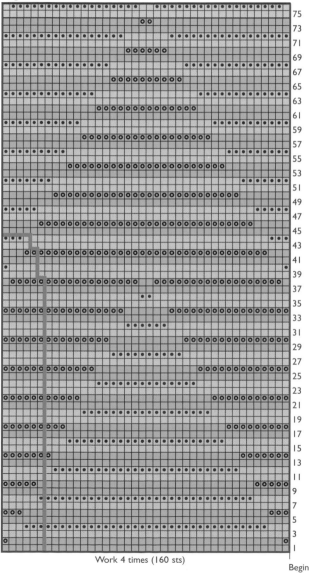

Work 4 times (160 sts)

Begin

Right Back, Rows 77–152

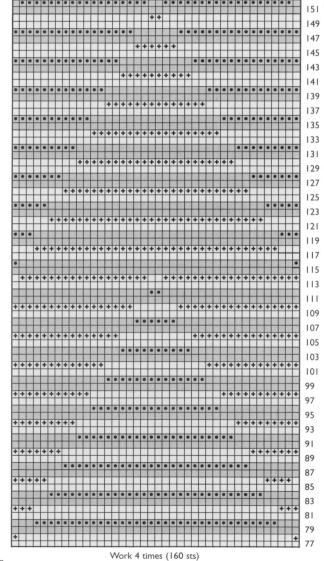

Work 4 times (160 sts)

new sts for band. Work as right front band, reversing shaping as foll:

Row 1: (WS) K1f&b in each of the first 2 sts, k2, p2, k2tog through back loop (tbl) (1 new st and 1 center front st) turn work—9 sts.

Row 2: (RS) Sl 1 pwise wyf, k2, p2, [sl 1 pwise wyf, k1] 2 times.

Row 3: (WS) [Sl 1 pwise wyf, k1] 2 times, k2, p2, k2tog tbl, turn.

Rep Rows 2 and 3 until all vertical sts along front edge have been worked, ending with a RS row—9 band sts rem (along with 170 sts around neck). Cont as foll:

Row 1: (WS) Using cir needle and yarn attached to neck-band sts, work left front band sts as foll: [Sl 1 pwise

Right Front, Rows 1–76

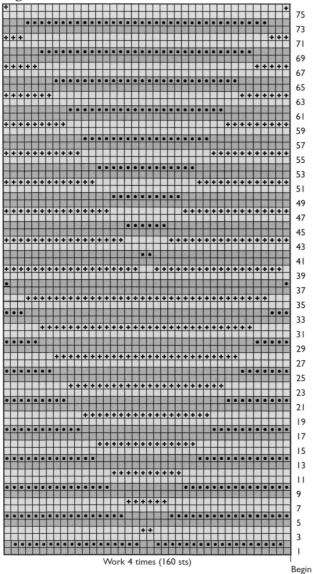

Work 4 times (160 sts)

Begin

Right Front, Rows 77–152

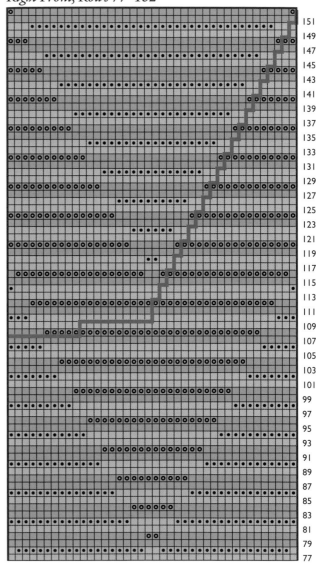

Work 4 times (160 sts)

Left Front, Rows 1–76

Left Front, Rows 77–152

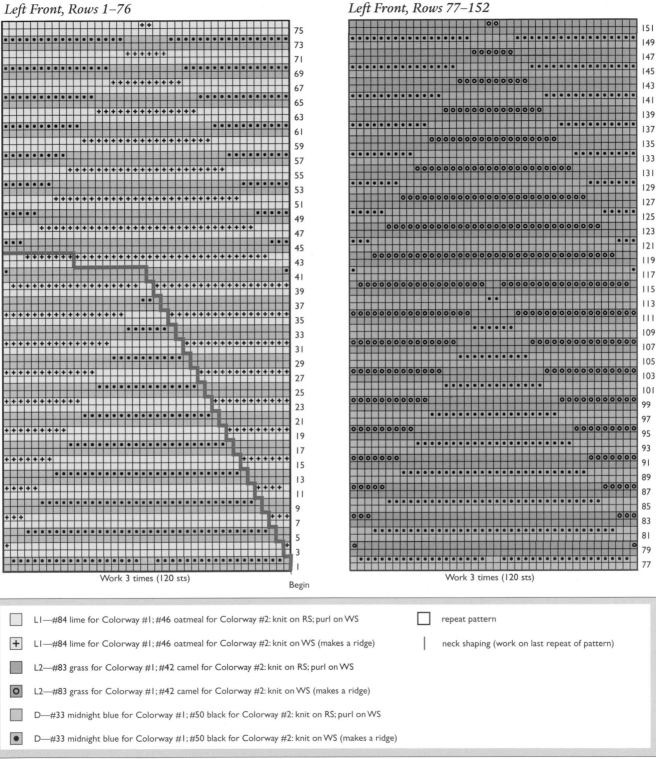

Work 3 times (120 sts)

Begin

Work 3 times (120 sts)

L1—#84 lime for Colorway #1; #46 oatmeal for Colorway #2: knit on RS; purl on WS

+   L1—#84 lime for Colorway #1; #46 oatmeal for Colorway #2: knit on WS (makes a ridge)

L2—#83 grass for Colorway #1; #42 camel for Colorway #2: knit on RS; purl on WS

○   L2—#83 grass for Colorway #1; #42 camel for Colorway #2: knit on WS (makes a ridge)

D—#33 midnight blue for Colorway #1; #50 black for Colorway #2: knit on RS; purl on WS

•   D—#33 midnight blue for Colorway #1; #50 black for Colorway #2: knit on WS (makes a ridge)

repeat pattern

| neck shaping (work on last repeat of pattern)

wyf, k1] 2 times, k2, p2, p2tog tbl (9th st of neckband and the first st on cir needle—left front band is now worked on 8 sts), knit to end of neckband sts (forms a ridge on the RS), and *at the same time* dec 14 sts evenly spaced across back neck, end row by working the last 8 sts in established patt for the right front band—148 sts plus 8 sts for each front band.

Rows 2–6: Work 8-st front band as established, work St st to last 8 sts, work 8-st band as established.

Cut yarn, leaving a 4" (10-cm) tail. Place 8 sts from each front band on separate holders—148 neckband sts rem.

Inside neckband

With WS of jacket facing and using a second ball of yarn, pick up and knit 1 st in each of the loops previously picked up around neck—53 sts from center front to shoulder seam, 1 st in right shoulder seam, 54 sts across back neck, 1 st in left shoulder seam, and 53 sts to left center front—162 neckband sts. Working an edge st at each end of needle (see Notes), knit 1 row to form a ridge on RS of inside neckband, and *at the same time* dec 14 sts evenly spaced across back neck—148 neckband sts rem. Knit 1 row, purl 1 row, knit 1 row. Cut second ball of yarn. *Next row:* (WS) With WS facing, cont with original yarn attached to work, place one 8-st border on each end of cir needle.

Join inside and outside neckband

Hold both cir needles tog with WS of neckbands facing each other. Work sts from both needles tog as foll: Work 8-st border as established, *k2tog (1 st from each needle); rep from * to last 8 sts (forms a ridge on the RS), work 8-st border as established.

Collar

From this point, the border continues upward on both sides and the St sts of the neckband become the collar. Beg with a RS row, work 8-st border as established, work p2, k2 rib across 148 neckband sts, work 8-st border as established. Cont in this manner until collar measures about ⅜" (1 cm) from joining row. Change to size 2 (3-mm) cir needle and cont in established patt, working 2 more buttonholes along right front edge of band at about the same spacing as the previous buttonholes, then work ⅜" (1 cm) more in patt—collar should measure about 8" (20.5 cm) high. With WS facing, BO all sts in patt.

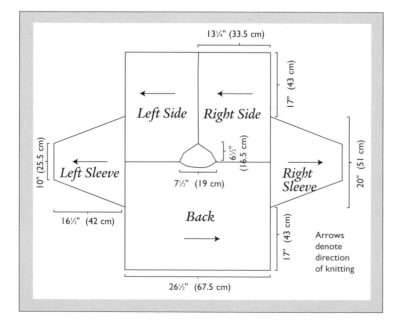

Buttons

With sewing needle threaded with matching thread, sew buttons to left front border and collar, opposite buttonholes. The buttons on the collar are sewn on the RS, and are not visible when collar is folded over.

FINISHING

Seams: Remove the waste yarn from the 101 sts below the underarm marker of the left front side edge and 101 sts of the left back side edge, and place the sts onto two smaller cir needles (101 sts on each needle). With RS tog, join L2 and with larger needle and using the three-needle method (see Techniques, page 135) BO the sts tog. With D, use the three-needle method to BO right front and back sts the same way. Using the mattress st and carefully matching stripes, sew sleeve seams, leaving the lower 4″ (10 cm) open. Try on jacket and decide how long the sleeves should be. Unravel or knit more rows until sleeves are desired length. Leave sts on needle.

Sleeve edgings: Turn sleeve so WS is facing. Using the outermost right st as the beg st, with D and using the knitted method, CO 9. Beg with Row 3, work sleeve edging as for right front band (omitting buttonholes, of course) until all sts around lower sleeve edge have been worked—9 band sts rem. Using the Kitchener st (see Techniques, page 139) graft live band sts to CO edge of band. Sew rem 4″ (10 cm) of sleeve seam.

Weave in all loose ends to WS and secure.

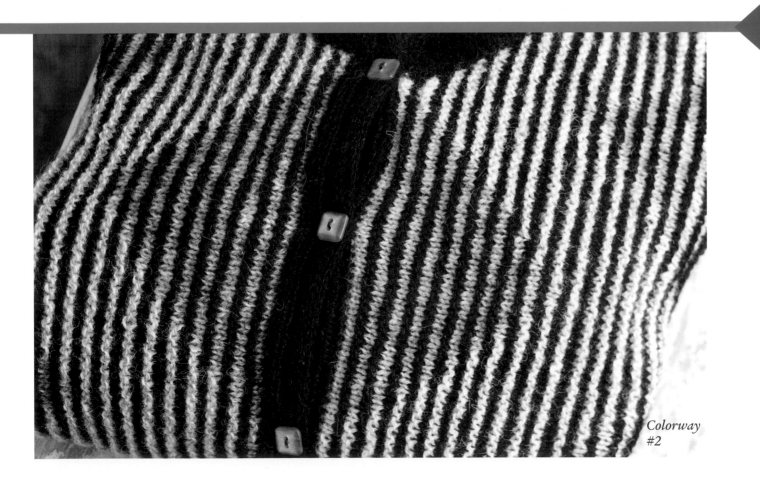

Colorway #2

FINISHED SIZE
44 (48, 52)" (112 [122,
132] cm) bust/chest circumference. Sweater shown
measures 48" (122 cm).

YARN

Fingering-weight yarn.
Sweater requires about 865
(1085, 1300) yd (790 [992,
1189] m) dark yarn (D), 645
(865, 865) yd (589 [790,
790] m) light yarn (L1), and
217 yd (198 m) each of two
other light yarns (L2 and L3).
We suggest Harrisville
Designs New England
Shetland (100% pure virgin
wool; 217 yd [198 m]/50 g):
#19 blackberry (D), 4 (5, 6)
skeins; #65 chianti, (L1) 3 (4,
4) skeins; #65 poppy (L2)
and #80 foliage (L3), 1 skein
each.

NEEDLES

Sizes 1 and 2 (2.5 mm and
3 mm): 24" (60-cm) circular
(cir); size 1 (2.5 mm): set of
2 double-pointed (dpn).
Adjust needle size if necessary
to obtain the correct gauge.

NOTIONS

Markers (m); tapestry needle.

GAUGE

24 sts and 46 rows = 4"
(10 cm) in charted pattern.

SAWTOOTH SWEATER

*Knit from cuff to cuff (right side to left side) using four colors,
this stylish sweater features diagonal shadow stripes, and
pointed or "sawtooth" edgings at the collar and cuffs.*

NOTES

Before beginning, review Tips—Before
You Knit, pages 11–14; Abbreviations,
page 134; Techniques, pages 135–140.

This sweater is worked sideways in one
piece, beginning with the right sleeve,
across the front and back, then down the
left sleeve. A schematic is on page 122.

The chart for this sweater is on page 124.
It is a modified diagonal pattern, with the
shadow pattern slanting to the right.
There is one edge stitch worked at each
side of garment; edge stitches are not
shown on chart. Work edge stitches as
follows: slip 1 knitwise at beginning of
every row and purl 1 at end of every row.

The yarn for this sweater can be purchased as a kit. See Resources, page 142
for more information.

RIGHT SLEEVE

Sawtooth edging
The cuff is worked sideways in a sawtooth
pattern. With D and dpn, CO 12 sts.
Row 1: (WS) Knit to last st, p1.
Row 2: (RS) Sl 1 kwise, k1, pick up and

knit 1 st in strand between sts as for a
M1 increase (see Techniques, page
138), but do not twist the strand (pro-
duces a small decorative hole), knit to
last st, p1—13 sts.
Row 3: Sl 1 kwise, knit to last st, p1.
Rows 4–13: Rep Rows 2 and 3 five more
times—18 sts on needle.
Row 14: (RS) BO 6 sts, knit to last st, p1—
12 sts rem; 1 point at cuff edge completed; 7 garter ridges worked.
Rep Rows 1–14 until there are 6 (6, 7)
points (piece should fit snugly around
the wrist), and BO *all* sts on final rep of
Row 14. Cut yarn.

Faux roll
With L3, dpn, and RS facing, pick up
and knit 1 st in each edge st along long,
straight side of edging—42 (42, 49) sts.
Knit 1 row on WS, purl 1 row on RS,
knit 1 row on WS. *Inc row:* (RS) Knit, inc
18 (20, 15) sts evenly spaced—60 (62,
64) sts; 58 (60, 62) patt sts, plus 1 edge
st at each end of needle (edge sts are not
shown on chart; see Notes). Place marker at center of row and keep in place
throughout the work. Break yarn. Do
not turn work.

Sleeve body

With RS still facing, join L1, change to larger cir needle, and work as foll (this will be a second RS row and worked immediately after the RS inc row): Sl 1 kwise (edge st), beg and end as indicated for your size, work next 58 (60, 62) sts according to Row 1 of Sawtooth Sweater chart (page 124), p1 (edge st). Working 1 edge st each end, work through Row 12 (10, 8) of chart. *Next row:* Sl 1 kwise (edge st), M1, work next 58 (60, 62) sts according to Row 13 (11, 9) of chart, M1, p1 (edge st). Working new sts into patt, work through Row 64 of chart (shadow pattern will shift to the right as work progresses), and *at the same time* cont to shape sleeve as foll: Inc 1 st each end of needle every foll 8 (8, 6)th row 7 (2, 30) times, then every 6 (6, 4)th row 21 (28, 2) times—118 (124, 130) sts (including edge sts) after all incs have been worked. *Note:* Not all sleeve incs are shown on chart due to page size restriction. Cont even in patt until a total of 196 (200, 200) rows of Sawtooth Sweater chart have been worked (not including edging), ending with a WS row.

BACK AND FRONT

Right shoulder

With RS facing, join L1, place marker (pm) at beg of sleeve sts to identify underarm, work across 118 (124, 130) sleeve sts, pm to identify other underarm. Using the backward loop method (see Techniques, page 135), CO 99 (106, 113) sts for back—158 (168, 178) sts total from center sleeve marker. *Next Row:* (WS) Working the new sts into established patt (see Tips—Before You Knit, page 12), work the 99 (106, 113) CO sts, then work 118 (124, 130) sleeve sts as established, then use the backward loop method to CO 99 (106, 113) sts for front—158 (168, 178) sts from center marker; 316 (336, 356) sts total. Slip center marker each row to identify center of garment. The first 10 and last 10 sts of each row are the bottom edges of the front and back, and are worked every row as foll: Sl 1 kwise, k9 (10 edge sts), work to last 10 sts in established patt,

k9, p1 (10 edge sts). Cont as established for 88 (98, 110) rows, counting from first row of CO sts for body.

Shape front neck

Note: The WS rows of the Neckline chart (page 125) are shaded gold to help distinguish RS and WS rows. As you work the chart, follow the pink or green line for the neck shaping, and work the other sts in the established patts and colors. *Next row:* (RS) With L1 (D, D), work 158 (168, 178) front sts to center marker, place rem 158 (168, 178) back sts on holder to work later. Cont in patt as established, shape front neck according to Neckline chart as foll: With WS facing, BO 5 (7, 7) sts, work to end. Work 1 RS row even. At neck edge (beg of WS rows), BO 4 (6, 6) sts 2 (1, 1) time(s), then BO 2 sts 2 times—141 (151, 161) sts rem. BO 1 st at beg of next 4 (8, 8) WS rows—137 (143, 153) sts rem. Work 3 rows even in patt. BO 1 st at beg of next WS row—136 (142, 152) sts rem. Work even in patt for 35 (25, 25) more rows, ending with a RS row. *Next row:* (WS) Using the knitted method (see Techniques, page 136), CO 1 st, work in patt to end of row—137 (143, 153) sts. Work 3 rows even in patt. Working new sts into established patt, CO 1 st at beg of next 4 (8, 8) WS rows—141

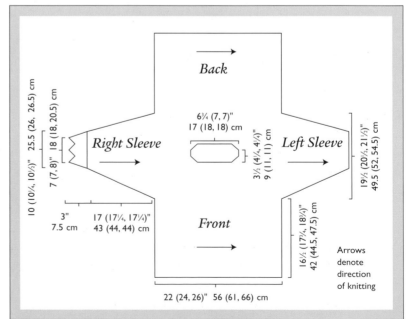

(151, 161) sts. CO 2 sts at beg of next 2 WS rows, then CO 4 (6, 6) sts at beg of next 2 (1, 1) WS row(s), then CO 5 (7, 7) sts at beg of foll WS row—158 (168, 178) sts. Place front sts on holder to work later.

Shape back neck

Return 158 (168, 178) held back sts onto cir needle. Join L1 (D, D), shape back neck as foll: (RS) BO 4 sts at beg of neck edge row, work to end—154 (164, 174) sts rem. Work 3 (1, 1) row(s) even. BO 1 st at beg of next RS row—153 (163, 173) sts rem. *For sizes M and L only:* Work 3 rows even, then BO 1 st at beg of next RS row—153 (162, 172) sts rem. *For all sizes:* Work even in patt for 67 (65, 65) rows. Using the knitted method, CO 1 st at beg of next RS row. Work 3 rows even. *For sizes M and L only:* CO 1 st at beg of next RS row, then work 1 row even. *For all sizes:* CO 4 sts at beg of next RS row—158 (168, 178) sts. Work 1 WS row even. Cut yarns.

Left shoulder

With RS facing, place 158 (168, 178) front sts and 158 (168, 178) back sts onto same needle to rejoin front and back—316 (336, 356) sts total. Join D at beg of lower front edge and cont even in patt as established for 86 (96, 108) rows, ending with a WS row. BO 99 (106, 113) sts at beg of next 2 rows—118 (124, 130) sts rem (including edge sts); 88 (98, 110) rows from completion of neckline.

LEFT SLEEVE

Note: In the foll sleeve shaping, decs are worked on both RS and WS rows. To maintain consistent appearance of the decs, work ssk at the beg of RS rows, k2tog at end of RS rows; work ssp at beg of WS rows, p2tog at end of WS rows (see Techniques, page 137).

Work 1 (5, 3) row(s) in established patts and colors. *Next Row:* Sl 1 kwise (edge st), dec 1 st (see Note), work in patt to last 3 sts, dec 1 st, p1 (edge st)—2 sts decreased. Cont to dec 1 st each end of needle in this manner every 6 (6, 4)th row 21 (28, 2) times, then every foll 8 (8, 6)th row 7 (2, 30)

times—60 (62, 64) sts rem (including edge sts). Work 12 (10, 8) rows even—196 (200, 200) rows.

Faux roll

Change to smaller needle and join L3. Cont in patt, with RS facing, knit 1 row, dec 18 (20, 15) sts evenly spaced—42 (42, 49) sts rem. With dpn and L3, knit 1 WS row. Purl 1 RS row. Knit 1 WS row, turn work.

Sawtooth edging

Note: All RS rows end with p2tog; all WS rows begin with sl 1 kwise (this will be the innermost st next to the sleeve sts). With D, dpn, RS facing, and working into the first st on left needle, use the knitted method to CO 12 new sts.

Row 1: (RS) Working the new CO sts, k2, pick up and knit 1 st in the strand between the last st worked and the next st, knit to last CO st, p2tog (1 st from CO sts and 1 sleeve st)—13 sts.

Rows 2, 4, 6, 8, 10, and 12: (WS) Sl 1 kwise, knit to last st, p1.

Rows 3, 5, 7, 9, and 11: (RS) Sl 1 kwise, k1, pick up and knit 1 st in strand between sts, knit to last st, p2tog (1 st from CO sts and 1 sleeve st)—18 sts rem after Row 11.

Row 13: (RS) BO 6 sts, knit to last st, p2tog—12 sts rem.

Row 14: (WS) Sl 1 kwise, knit to last st, p1—1 point at cuff edge completed; 7 garter ridges worked.

Rep Rows 1–14 (working Row 1 same as Row 3 in all subsequent reps) until there are 6 (6, 7) points. BO *all* sts on final rep of Row 14. Cut yarn.

FINISHING

Seams: Fold garment in half so that RS of front and back face out, matching underarm markers. With D threaded on a tapestry needle and using the invisible horizontal seam (see Techniques, page 139), sew side seams. With RS tog and D, sew cuff edges tog. Turn sleeve to RS and sew sleeve seam.

Neck edging: With L3, smaller cir needle, RS facing, and beg at right shoulder, pick up and knit 63 sts along front neck edge and 63 sts along back neck edge—126 sts total. Join for working in the rnd. *Faux roll:* Purl 3 rnds. Change to D and knit 1 rnd. *Sawtooth edging:* With dpn, using the knitted method, and working into the first st of the rnd, CO 12 new sts with D. Work sawtooth edging as for left sleeve cuff until all neck sts have been joined to edging. BO all edging sts. With RS of edging facing tog, sew BO edge to CO edge.

Remove markers, weave in all loose ends to WS.

Sawtooth Sweater

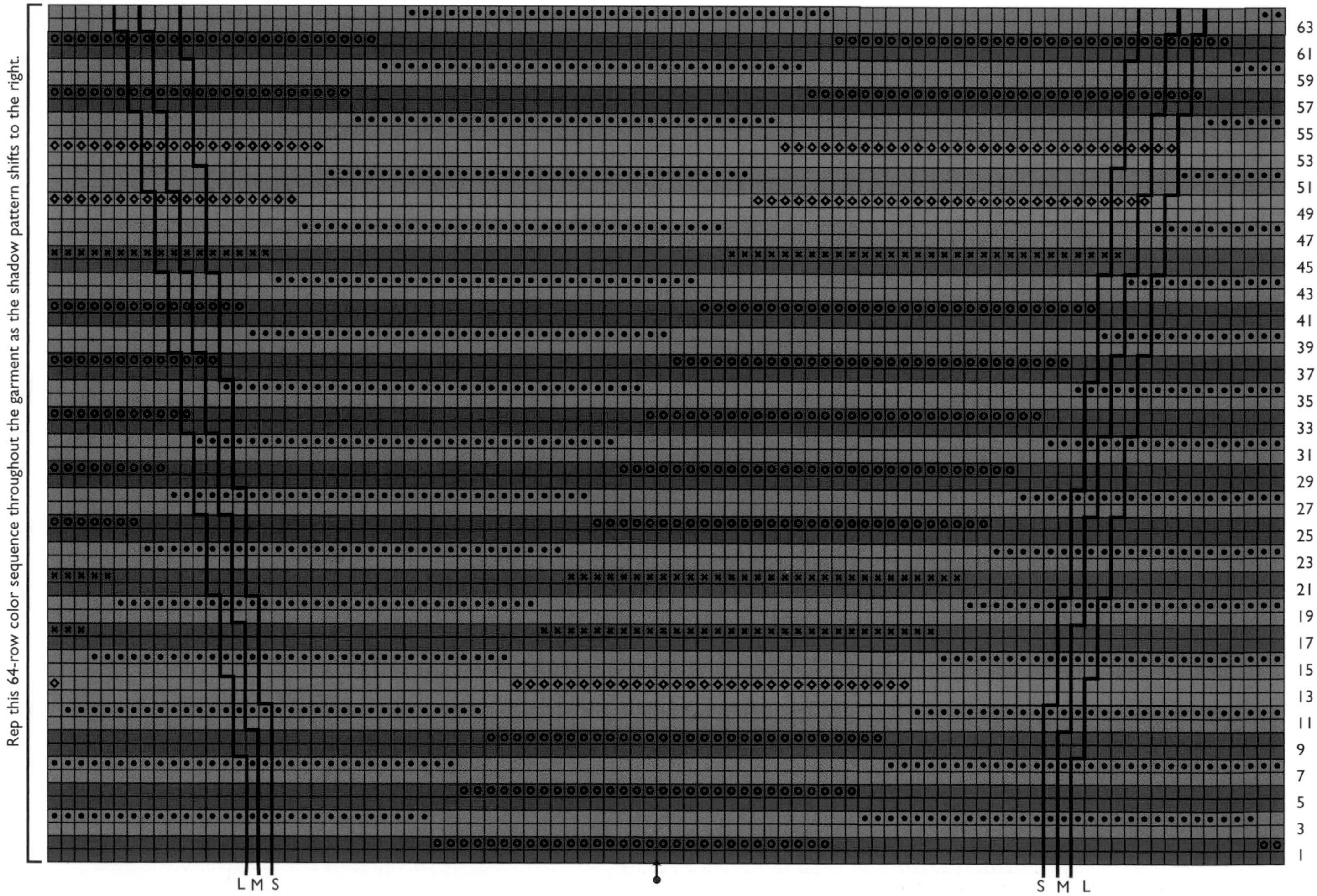

Sleeves: Edge sts are not shown on chart. The 64-row color sequence is repeated throughout the garment and the shadow pattern shifts to the right. Begin sleeves as shown here to set up color sequence, then follow text instructions for entire sleeve.

Neckline

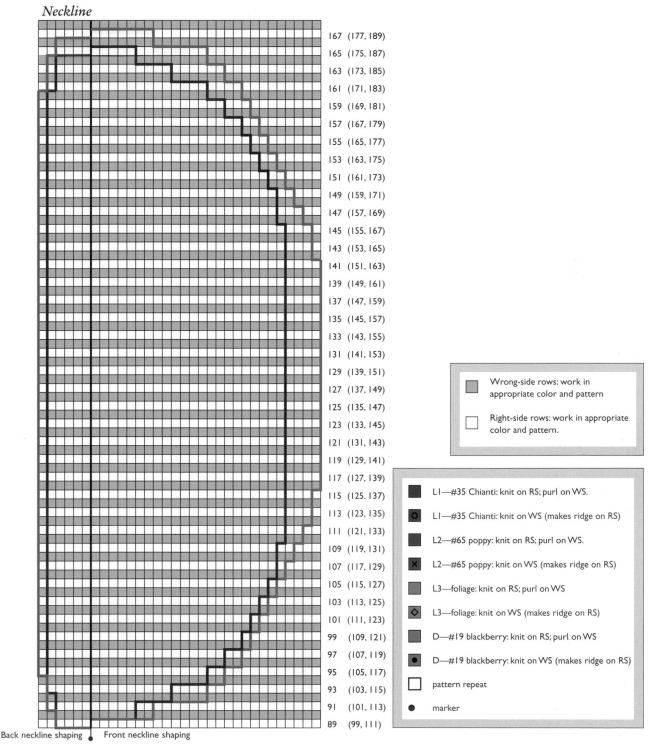

167 (177, 189)
165 (175, 187)
163 (173, 185)
161 (171, 183)
159 (169, 181)
157 (167, 179)
155 (165, 177)
153 (163, 175)
151 (161, 173)
149 (159, 171)
147 (157, 169)
145 (155, 167)
143 (153, 165)
141 (151, 163)
139 (149, 161)
137 (147, 159)
135 (145, 157)
133 (143, 155)
131 (141, 153)
129 (139, 151)
127 (137, 149)
125 (135, 147)
123 (133, 145)
121 (131, 143)
119 (129, 141)
117 (127, 139)
115 (125. 137)
113 (123, 135)
111 (121, 133)
109 (119, 131)
107 (117, 129)
105 (115, 127)
103 (113, 125)
101 (111, 123)
99 (109, 121)
97 (107, 119)
95 (105, 117)
93 (103, 115)
91 (101, 113)
89 (99, 111)

Back neckline shaping Front neckline shaping

center marker

Begin with green line for all sizes, then follow pink line for S, or green line for M and L

	Legend
▦ (gray)	Wrong-side rows: work in appropriate color and pattern
☐ (white)	Right-side rows: work in appropriate color and pattern.

■	L1—#35 Chianti: knit on RS; purl on WS.
⊙	L1—#35 Chianti: knit on WS (makes ridge on RS)
■	L2—#65 poppy: knit on RS; purl on WS.
⊠	L2—#65 poppy: knit on WS (makes ridge on RS)
▦	L3—foliage: knit on RS; purl on WS
◈	L3—foliage: knit on WS (makes ridge on RS)
■	D—#19 blackberry: knit on RS; purl on WS
⊙	D—#19 blackberry: knit on WS (makes ridge on RS)
☐	pattern repeat
●	marker

FINISHED SIZE

44 (48, 50, 53, 56)" (112 [122, 127, 134.5, 142] cm) bust/chest circumference. Kimonos shown measure 48" (122 cm).

YARN

Sport-weight yarn. Kimono requires about 1008 (1008, 1008, 1134, 1134) yd (922 [922, 922, 1037, 1037] m) dark yarn (D), 651 (651, 651, 868, 868) yd (595 [595, 595, 794, 794] m) of one light yarn (L1), and 434 (434, 651, 651, 651) yd (397 [397, 595, 595, 595] m) of another light yarn (L2).

We used: Colorway #1: Harrisville Designs, New England Shetland (100% pure virgin wool; 217 yd [198 m]/50 g): #18 aubergine (D), 5 (5, 5, 6, 6) skeins; #24 periwinkle (L1), 3 (3, 3, 4, 4) skeins; #72 lilac (L2), 2 (2, 3, 3, 3) skeins. Colorway #2: Dale of Norway Tiur (60% mohair, 40% wool; 126 yd [115 m]/50 g): dark green (D), 8 (8, 8, 9, 9) balls; jade green (L1), 6 (6, 6, 7, 7) balls; gold (L2), 4 (4, 4, 5, 5) balls.

NEEDLES

Size 1 and 2 (2.5 mm and 3 mm): 32" (80-cm) circular (cir). Adjust needle size if necessary to obtain the correct gauge.

NIHON JAPANESE KIMONO

. . . .

This handsome jacket features Japanese kimono shaping. It is shown here in two colorways and two different yarns.

NOTES

Before beginning, review Tips—Before You Knit, pages 11–14; Abbreviations, page 134; Techniques, pages 135–140.

The construction of this kimono jacket is similar to that of the Rainbow Jacket (page 88); it is worked sideways in two pieces. Each piece begins at the cuff and is worked to the center body, with stitches cast on to form one half of the front and one half of the back. The two halves are grafted together at the center back, and a garter-stitch band is added to the two center fronts and around the back neck.

The garment is worked back and forth in rows. A circular needle is used to accommodate the large number of stitches.

Always work 1 edge stitch at each side of the piece, even if not specifically mentioned in the instructions or shown on the charts. Work edge stitches as follows: slip 1 knitwise at the beginning of every row and purl 1 at the end of every row.

All increases are made by knitting into the front and back of a stitch (k1f&b).

Instructions are given for the small size with the larger sizes in parentheses. When only one number or set of instructions is given, it applies to all sizes.

Yarn for the violet colorway (Colorway #1) can be purchased as a kit. See Resources, page 142, for more information.

RIGHT HALF

Sleeve

With D and larger cir needle, CO 58 (60, 62, 64, 66) sts—1 edge st each end of needle and 56 (58, 60, 62, 64) main sts. Working back and forth in rows and working edge sts as described in Notes, knit 11 (11, 11, 13, 13) rows. *Note:* All five sizes are shown on the chart on page 132; the smallest size is innermost on the chart, the largest is outermost, and the rem sizes are in between. Each size begins on a different WS row after the cuff is finished.

Colorway #1

NOTIONS

Markers (m); 2 or 3 strands of smooth cotton yarn, about 1 yd (1 meter) each, to use as stitch holders; tapestry needle; decorative pin for jacket closing.

GAUGE

24 sts and 46 rows = 4" (10 cm) in charted pattern on larger needles.

Next row: (RS) Change to L1 (L1, L2, L2, L1) and knit, inc 1 st each side as foll: Sl 1 kwise (edge st), k1f&b, knit to last 2 sts, k1f&b, p1 (edge st)—2 sts inc'd; 60 (62, 64, 66, 68) sts. This row is not marked on the Kimono chart (pages 132–133), but counts as a RS row. Beg with a WS row as indicated for your size along left edge of chart, work chart from left to right on WS rows and right to left on RS rows to top of chart, then rep the top 44 rows of the chart pattern up and outwards—the patt will form diagonal stripes on each side of sleeve center. *At the same time,* inc 1 st each side of needle every 6th row 25 (23, 21, 19, 17) times, then every 4th row 7 (10, 13, 16, 19) times—124 (128, 132, 136, 140) sts. Cont even until a total of 182 rows of charted patt have been worked—piece should measure about 16¾" (42.5 cm) from CO. Place 3 markers on the last row to indicate each side edge of the sleeve underarm and the sleeve center. Do not BO.

Right Half Body

At beg of the next 2 rows, use the knitted method (see Techniques, page 136) to CO 88 (94, 100, 106, 112) sts

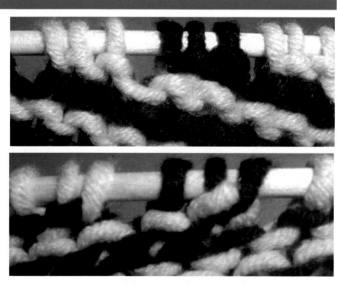

The yarnovers worked for short rows will cause the stitches on the needle to gather into groups of two stitches and one yarnover each. The right side is shown at top; the wrong side is at bottom.

(work the new sts at the beg of each row)—150 (158, 166, 174, 182) sts on each side of sleeve center marker; 300 (316, 332, 348, 364) sts total. Keep the center sleeve marker in place as you will need to refer to it later. Cont in patt as established, and *at the same time* establish garter-st borders on the first 10 and last 10 sts as foll: Sl 1 kwise, k9 (10 border sts), place marker (pm), work center 280 (296, 312, 328, 344) sts in established patt, pm, k9, p1 (10 border sts). *Note:* The border sts are not shown on chart.

Cont as established until piece measures about 8¼ (9, 9½, 10¼, 11)" (21 [23, 24, 26, 28] cm) from center sleeve marker, ending with two L1 rows—96 (104, 112, 120, 128) patt rows total.

Shape neck

Hold piece with RS facing so that sleeve edge is toward you, back/front is furthest from you, right front sts are on the right side of the marker, and the right side of the back sts are on the left side of the marker.

With cotton yarn threaded on a tapestry needle, thread through 1 st from the back (left side) and 21 sts from the front—22 sts total. Set these sts aside until later.

Back

Follow patt to the center back, and *at the same time* dec 1 st at neck edge at beg of every other row 2 times, then every 4th row 2 times, then every 8th row once—144 (152, 160, 168, 176) sts rem. Cont even until there are a total of 32 rows (5 ridges with L2; 3 ridges with L1) from beg of neck shaping (all sizes)—right half of back is now complete. Place these sts on waste yarn holder. Cut yarns, leaving 4" (10-cm) tails. Secure ends on WS.

Right front

Cont in patt, shape right front neck as foll: On RS rows at neck edge, shape neck with short rows by leaving 2 sts unworked at each short-row turn as foll: Work RS row 2 sts before neck edge, turn, yo, work to end of WS row. Rep

Colorway #2

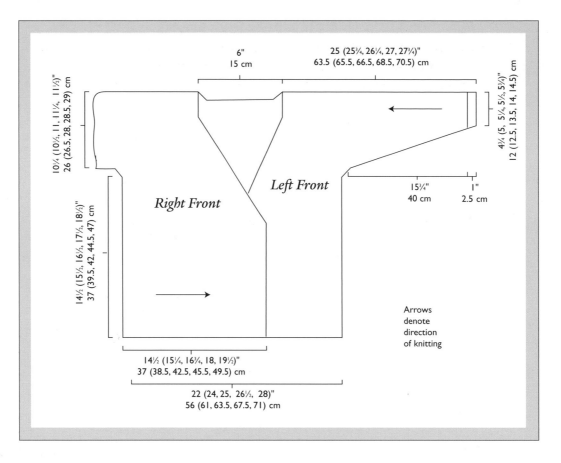

6"
15 cm

25 (25¾, 26¼, 27, 27¾)"
63.5 (65.5, 66.5, 68.5, 70.5) cm

10¼ (10½, 11, 11¼, 11½)"
26 (26.5, 28, 28.5, 29) cm

4¾ (5, 5¼, 5½, 5¾)"
12 (12.5, 13.5, 14, 14.5) cm

Left Front

Right Front

15¾"
40 cm

1"
2.5 cm

14½ (15¼, 16½, 17½, 18½)"
37 (39.5, 42, 44.5, 47) cm

Arrows
denote
direction
of knitting

14½ (15¼, 16¾, 18, 19½)"
37 (38.5, 42.5, 45.5, 49.5) cm

22 (24, 25, 26½, 28)"
56 (61, 63.5, 67.5, 71) cm

this short row, adding 2 more sts for neck each RS row until 67 working sts rem (not including the sts and yarnovers used in the short rows) and piece measures about 13 (13¾, 15¼, 16½, 18)" (33 [35, 38.5, 42, 45.5] cm) from side seam to center front.

CENTER FRONT

Note: For the center front border, use the same color sequence as used for the light colors in the preceding stripe. If L1 is the light color in use when piece measures the appropriate length from side edge to center front, then continue using L1 with D for the center front border. Likewise, if L2 is the light color at this point, continue using L2 with D for the center front border.

Cont to work in short rows, setting aside 2 sts for the neck on RS rows. Beg with the 67 working sts, work in dark and light stripes to form the center front edges, alternating 2 rows in D and 2 rows in L, and with 1 edge st at the lower edge until there are 8 ridges on the RS (4 ridges each of D and L). Finish with 2 more rows D. With D, BO rem stripe sts. Place short-row neck sts and yarnovers on holder.

LEFT HALF

The left side of the jacket corresponds to the right, except it is worked in reverse order. Work as for right side to end of neck shaping (page 128).

Set aside 1 st from back (right side of marker) and 21 sts from front on a cotton thread or holder for the neck. Next, work the left front as for the right front. Remember, the front is now on the left side of the center marker. This time, the color changes will occur at the neck edge when the work is turned. Be careful as you change colors that the color stranding doesn't draw in the stitches. The back is also worked as for the right side. Finish with 1 row with D (note that 13 rows are worked here instead of 12 as on the other side). Leave a very long tail of D for seaming.

FINISHING

With long tail threaded on a tapestry needle and using the Kitchener st (see Techniques, page 139), graft the two pieces together along the center back.

Neck edge and kimono collar: Place all held front sts and yarnovers, and back neck sts onto smaller cir needle—303 (329, 355, 381, 407) sts total. With D, RS facing, and beg at right front, knit across the right front sts working each yo tog with the st after it, then knit even across 29 (31, 33, 35, 37) back neck sts, then knit across the left front sts, working each yo tog with the st that comes after it through the back loop—227 (245, 263, 299) sts rem. With WS facing, knit 1 row even with D (making a ridge on RS).

Add sts for band width as foll: With D, RS facing, and using the knitted method, CO 10 sts at beg of row.
Row 1: (RS) K9, p2tog (1 st of band and 1 st of neck edge).
Row 2: (WS) Sl 1 kwise, k8, p1.
Rep these 2 rows until all body sts have been worked and only 10 sts rem for band, ending with a RS row. With WS facing, loosely BO all sts kwise.

Seams: With yarn threaded on a tapestry needle and using the mattress st (see Techniques, page 140), sew sleeve seams, carefully matching stripes. Sew side seams. Alternately, you can use the three-needle BO method to join the side seams (before sewing the sleeve seams) as foll: With smaller needles, pick up but do not knit 88 (94, 100, 106, 112) sts evenly spaced along each side edge (simply pick up loops and place them on the needle). Hold the pieces with RS facing each other, and with a larger needle and yarn to match the side edges, use the three-needle method (see Techniques, page 135) to loosely BO the sts tog. Weave in all loose ends to WS and secure. Remove all waste yarns and markers. Block to measurements (see schematic).

Kimono

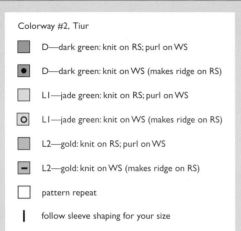

Colorway #2, Tiur

- D—dark green: knit on RS; purl on WS
- D—dark green: knit on WS (makes ridge on RS)
- L1—jade green: knit on RS; purl on WS
- L1—jade green: knit on WS (makes ridge on RS)
- L2—gold: knit on RS; purl on WS
- L2—gold: knit on WS (makes ridge on RS)
- pattern repeat
- | follow sleeve shaping for your size

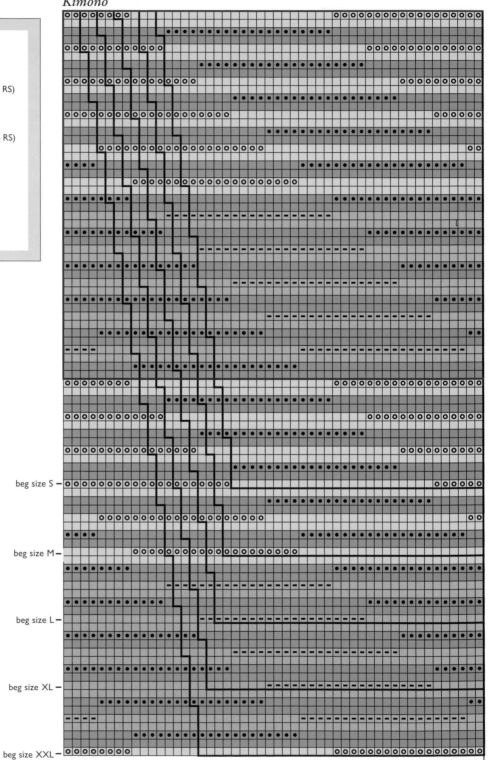

beg size S

beg size M

beg size L

beg size XL

beg size XXL

sleeve center

sleeve center

ABBREVIATIONS

beg	beginning, begin; begins
bet	between
BO	bind off
CC	contrasting color
cir	circular
cm	centimeter(s)
CO	cast on
cont	continue; continuing
D	dark color
dec(s)	decrease(s); decreasing
dpn	double-pointed needles(s)
foll	following; follows
g	gram(s)
inc	increase; increasing
k	knit
k1f&b	knit into front and back loops of the same st
k2tog	knit 2 stitches together
kwise	knitwise
L	light color
m	marker
MC	main color
mm	millimeter
M1	make one. A single st increase. See Techniques, page 138.
p	purl
p2tog	purl 2 stitches together
patt(s)	patterns(s)

pm	place marker
psso	pass slipped stitch over last stitch worked
pwise	purlwise
rem	remain(s); remaining
rep	repeat; repeating
rev St st	reverse stockinette stitch
rnd(s)	round(s)
RS	right side
sl	slip
sl m	slip marker
ssk	sl 2 sts kwise, one at a time from the left needle to the right needle, insert left needle tip into fronts of both sts and knit together in this position
st(s)	stitch(es)
St st	stockinette stitch
tbl	through back loop
tog	together
WS	wrong side
wyb	with yarn in back
wyf	with yarn in front
yo	yarn over
*	repeat starting point (i.e., repeat from *)
**	repeat all instructions between asterisks
()	alternate measurements and/or instructions
[]	instructions that are to be worked as a group a specified number of times

TECHNIQUES

BIND-OFFS

Standard Bind-Off

Knit 1 stitch, *knit 1 stitch (2 stitches on right needle), insert left needle into first stitch on right needle (Figure 1), pass this stitch over the second stitch (Figure 2) and off the needle—one stitch remains on right needle and one stitch has been bound off (Figure 3). Repeat from *.

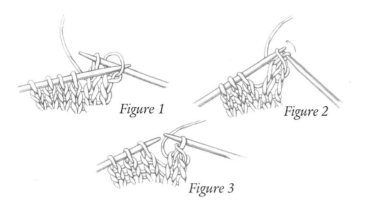

Figure 1

Figure 2

Figure 3

Three-Needle Bind-Off

Place stitches to be joined onto two separate needles. Unless otherwise directed, hold the needles together with right sides of knitting facing each other. *Insert a third needle into first stitch on each of the other two needles (Figure 1) and knit them together as one stitch (Figure 2). Knit next stitch on each needle the same way, then pass the first stitch over second stitch (Figure 3). Repeat from * until one stitch remains on third needle. Cut yarn and pull tail through last stitch.

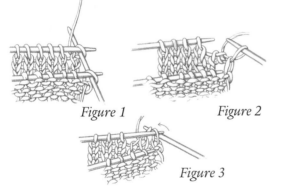

Figure 1

Figure 2

Figure 3

CAST-ONS

Backward Loop Cast-On

Loop working yarn and place on needle backward so that it doesn't unwind.

Knitted Cast-On

Place a slipknot on left needle if there are no established stitches. *With right needle, knit into first stitch (or slipknot) on left needle (Figure 1) and place new stitch onto left needle (Figure 2). Repeat from *, always knitting into last stitch made.

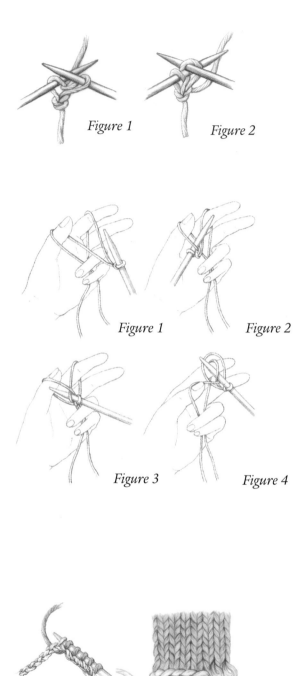

Figure 1   Figure 2

Long-Tail (Continental) Cast-On

Leaving a long tail (about ½″ to 1″ [1.3 cm to 2.5 cm] for each stitch to be cast on), make a slipknot and place on right needle. Place thumb and index finger of left hand between yarn ends so that the working yarn is draped over the index finger and the tail end is over the thumb. Secure both ends with your other fingers and hold palm upwards, making a V of yarn (Figure 1). Bring needle up through loop on thumb (Figure 2), grab first strand around index finger with needle, and go back down through loop on thumb (Figure 3). Drop loop off thumb and, placing thumb back in V configuration, tighten resulting stitch on needle (Figure 4).

Figure 1   Figure 2

Figure 3   Figure 4

Provisional Crochet Chain Cast-On

Using smooth, waste cotton yarn and a crochet hook, crochet a chain the number of stitches specified for the cast-on, plus a few extra stitches. Using the yarn and knitting needle specified in the instructions, pick up and knit a stitch through the bump on the back of a crochet chain for each stitch (Figure 1). This counts as the first row of the pattern. If desired, place a knot in the end of the waste yarn to identify where the cast-on chain ended. When you're ready to work in the opposite direction, remove the crochet chain by pulling the end with the knot through the last chain, then pulling on the waste yarn to remove the remaining chains (Figure 2), placing the exposed stitches on a knitting needle or stitch holder.

Figure 1   Figure 2

DECREASES

K2tog

Insert right needle tip into front of second stitch on left needle, then through the first stitch, and knit the two together as if they were a single stitch. This decrease leans to the right.

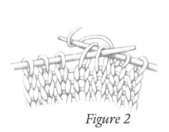

P2tog

Insert right needle tip into front of first stitch on left needle, then through the second stitch and purl the two together as if they were a single stitch. This decrease is typically worked on wrong-side rows and is equivalent to the k2tog decrease.

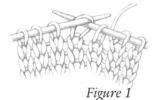

Figure 1

Figure 2

Ssk

Slip two stitches individually knitwise from the left needle to the right needle (Figure 1). Insert the tip of the left needle into the front loops of both of these stitches, then knit them together through their back loops (Figure 2). This decrease leans to the left.

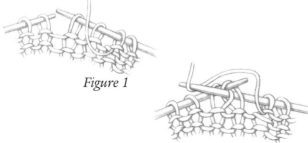

Figure 1

Figure 2

Ssp

Slip two stitches individually knitwise from the left needle to the right needle (Figure 1). Insert the tip of the left needle into the fronts of both stitches and slip them back to the left needle in their twisted orientation. Insert the right needle tip through the back loops of these stitches (going through the second, then the first), then purl them together through their back loops (Figure 2). This decrease is typically worked on wrong-side rows and is equivalent to the ssk decrease.

INCREASES

K1f&b

Knit into the front loop of a stitch as usual but do not slide the stitch off the left needle (Figure 1), then knit through the back loop of the same stitch (Figure 2).

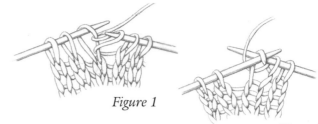

Figure 1

Figure 2

Make 1 (M1)

The Make 1 increase can be worked to form a right- or left-slanting increase. If you don't care which direction the increased stitch slants, use the method you prefer.

M1 RIGHT SLANT

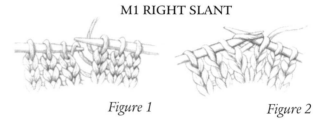

Figure 1   *Figure 2*

Right slant: Insert the left needle tip from back to front under the running strand between the last stitch on the right needle and the first stitch on the left needle (Figure 1). Knit the strand through the front loop to twist the stitch (Figure 2).

M1 LEFT SLANT

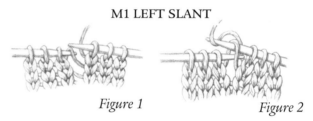

Figure 1   *Figure 2*

Left slant: Insert the left needle tip from front to back under the running strand between the last stitch on the right needle and the first stitch on the left needle (Figure 1). Knit the strand through the back loop to twist the stitch (Figure 2).

SEAMS

Backstitch Seam

Working from right to left, bring threaded needle up through both pieces of knitted fabric (Figure 1), then back down through both layers a stitch or two to the right of the starting point (Figure 2). *Bring needle up through both layers a stitch or two to the left of the stitch just made (Figure 3), then back down to the right, in the place used before (Figure 4). Repeat from *, working backward one stitch, then forward two stitches.

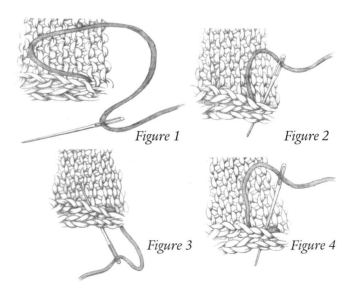

Figure 1   *Figure 2*

Figure 3   *Figure 4*

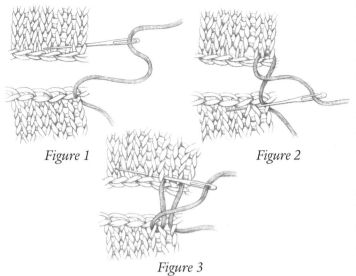

Figure 1

Figure 2

Figure 3

Invisible Horizontal Seam

Bring threaded needle out at the center of the first stitch on one piece, then in and out under the first whole stitch on the other piece (Figure 1). *Insert needle into the center of the same stitch it came out before, then out through the center of the adjacent stitch (Figure 2). Insert needle in and out through the next whole stitch on the other piece (Figure 3). Repeat from *, ending with a half-stitch on the first piece.

Kitchener Stitch Seam

The Kitchener stitch is used to invisibly join live stitches without binding them off. It is worked with yarn threaded on a tapestry needle. The yarn is guided through the live stitches in a manner that mimics a row of knitting. Place the live stitches to be joined on two separate needles and hold the needles parallel to each other with the wrong sides of the knitting facing each other. Beginning at the right-hand selvedge edge, work as follows, mimicking garter stitch or stockinette stitch, as desired.

GARTER STITCH

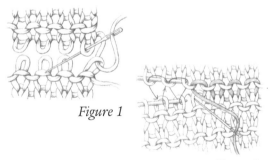

Figure 1

Figure 2

Garter Stitch:

Step 1: Bring threaded needle through the first front stitch as if to purl (purlwise).

Step 2: Bring threaded needle through the first back stitch purlwise (Figure 1).

Step 3: Bring threaded needle as if to knit (knitwise) through the same front stitch previously entered, then through the next front stitch purlwise.

Step 4: Bring threaded needle knitwise though the same back stitch previously entered, then through the next back stitch purlwise.

Repeat Steps 3 and 4 (Figure 2) until all stitches have been joined.

STOCKINETTE STITCH

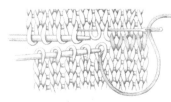

Stockinette Stitch:

Step 1: Bring threaded needle through the first front stitch as if to purl (purlwise).

Step 2: Bring threaded needle through the first back stitch as if to knit (knitwise).

Step 3: Bring threaded needle knitwise through same front stitch, then through next front stitch purlwise.

Step 4: Bring threaded needle though the back stitch as if to purl, then through the next back stitch knitwise (as shown in illustration).

Repeat Steps 3 and 4 until all stitches have been joined.

Mattress Stitch Seam

Lay the pieces to be seamed on a flat surface, with the right sides facing upward. Thread yarn on a tapestry needle and work as follows.

Garter Stitch:

*Insert threaded needle into the lower purl bar between the last two stitches on one piece (Figure 1), then upper purl bar from the stitch next to the edge stitch the bottom loop of the corresponding row on the other piece (Figure 2). Repeat from *. Pull the seaming yarn gently to draw the two pieces together after every stitch.

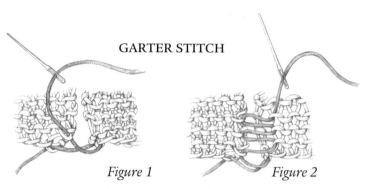

GARTER STITCH

Figure 1   *Figure 2*

Stockinette Stitch:

Insert threaded needle under one bar between first two stitches on one piece (Figure 1), then the corresponding bar plus the bar above it on the other piece (Figure 2). *Insert needle under the next two bars on the first piece, then next two bars on the other piece (Figure 3). Repeat from *, ending by picking up last the bar (or pair of bars) at the top of the first piece. Pull the seaming yarn gently to draw the two pieces together after every stitch.

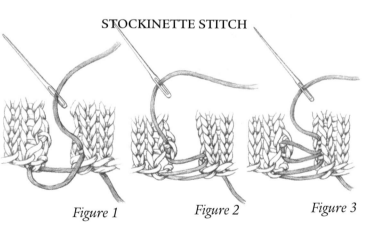

STOCKINETTE STITCH

Figure 1   *Figure 2*   *Figure 3*

Whipstitch Seam

Unless otherwise specified, hold the pieces to be seamed with right sides together. Working from right to left, *bring threaded needle from back to front through both layers. Repeat from *.

RESOURCES

YARNS

Information about yarns used in this book may be obtained from your local yarn shop, or from the following manufacturers/distributors.

Dale of Norway
www.dale.no
> Tiur (60% mohair, 40% wool; 126 yd [115 m]/50 g)

GGH Muench
www.muenchyarns.com
> Sierra (77% wool, 23% polyamid; 50 yd [45 m]/50 g)

Harrisville Designs, Inc.
www.harrisville.com
> New England Knitters Sheltand (100% pure virgin wool; 217 yd [198 m]/50 g)

HP Gruppen
www.hpgruppen.dk
> Cosy Wool (100% wool; 137 yd [125 m]/100 g)
> Kick (50% cotton, 50% acrylic; 164 yd [150 m]/50 g)

Noro Yarns
Distributed in the U.S. by Knitting Fever, Inc.
www.knittingfever.com
> Silk Garden (45% silk, 45% kid mohair, 10% wool; 110 yd [100 m]/50 g)

Rowan Yarns
www.knitrowan.com
> All Seasons Cotton (60% cotton, 40% acrylic; 99 yd [90 m]/50 g)
> Cotton Glacé (100% cotton; 126 yd [115 m]/50 g)
> 4-Ply Cotton (100% cotton; 186 yd [170 m]/50 g)
> Handknit DK Cotton (100% cotton; 93 yd [85 m]/50 g)
> Wool Cotton (50% merino wool, 50% cotton; 125 yd [113 m]/50 g)

KITS

The following designs may be ordered from Harrisville Designs as complete, ready-to-knit yarn packs containing enough Harrisville New England Shetland to complete the garment. Please specify the kit name and colorway in your order. Visit www.viv.dk for additional colorways.

Vivian Høxbro
www.viv.dk

Wholesale USA and Canada:
Harrisville Designs
Center Village, PO Box 806
Harrisville, NH 03450
USA
Telephone: (603) 827-3333
(800) 338-9415
Fax: (603) 827-3335
www.harrisville.com

Collared Jacket (page 110)
Kit name: H2340 Collared Jacket (Specify green colorway or gray-beige colorway)

Nihon Japanese Kimono (page 126)
Kit name: H2338 Nihon Japanese Kimono (violet colorway)

Ocean Vest (page 94)
Kit name: H2341 Ocean Vest

Rainbow Jacket (page 88)
Kit name: H2315 Rainbow Jacket

Sawtooth Sweater (page 120)
Kit name: H2339 Sawtooth Sweater

Tone-on-Tone (pages 78 and 84)
Kit name: H2337 Tone-on-Tone. Specify gray colorway (for Woman's version) or brown/golden colorway (for Man's version)

Wing Shawls
   Small Shawl (page 50)
   Kit name: H2334 Wing Shawl 1

   Triangles Shawl (page 52)
   Kit name: H2335 Wing Shawl 2 (Gray colorway)

   Diagonal Stripes Shawl (page 56)
   Kit name: H2336 Wing Shawl 3 (Red colorway)

INDEX

abbreviations 134

bind-offs 135
Block Pullover 72–77
Button Heart Bag 24–27

cast-ons 135–136
charts, reading 9, 10
circular knitting 14
Classic Cross Pillow 28–31
color 10, 12
Collared Jacket 110–119
counting rows 14

decreases 137
Diagonal Cross Pillow 32–37

edges 11
ends 13

Fur Heart Bag 20–23

garter stitch 139, 140
gauge 10, 11

Heart Top 42–47

increases 138

joining 14

Kitchener stitch 139
kits 142

markers 12, 13
Matching Hat and Scarf 38–41
mattress stitch 140

Nihon Japanese Kimono 126–133

Ocean Vest 94–101

patterning, shadow 6–8, 9
patterns, basic 7–8, 9, 12
Pot Holders 16–19

Rainbow Jacket 88–93
resources 141–142
rows, counting 14

Sawtooth Sweater 120–125
seams 139–140
sizes 14
Squared Top 64–71
stitches 135–140
stockinette stitch 139, 140
stripes 8, 9

techniques 135–140
tips 11–14
Tone-on-Tone Sweaters 78–87
Triangle Top 102–109

whipstitch 140
Wing Shawls 48–63

yarns 10